W. S. Weeden

Songs of the Peacemaker

A Collection of sacred songs and hymns for use in all services of the church,

Sunday-school

W. S. Weeden

Songs of the Peacemaker
A Collection of sacred songs and hymns for use in all services of the church, Sunday-school

ISBN/EAN: 9783337265649

Printed in Europe, USA, Canada, Australia, Japan

Cover: Foto ©Lupo / pixelio.de

More available books at **www.hansebooks.com**

Songs of the Peacemaker.

—BY—

W. S. WEEDEN,
GEO. BEAVERSON,
AND
LEONARD WEAVER,
(Evangelist).

A Compilation of Sacred Songs.

PUBLISHED BY
J. W. VAN DE VENTER & CO.,

NEW YORK:
W. S. WEEDEN,
441 PEARL ST.

PITTSBURG, PA.:
J. W. VAN DE VENTER,
805 LEWIS BLOCK.

CANADA AGENCY:
LEONARD WEAVER,
GRIMSBY, • • • • • • ONTARIO.

Single copies, by mail, 35 cents; per doz., not prepaid, $3.60; per hundred, $30.

Begin the Day with God.

FRANK MILLER.

1. Begin the day with God! He is the sun and day; He is the radiance of thy dawn; To Him ad-dress thy lay.
2. Take thy first walk with God! Let Him go forth with thee; By stream, or sea, or mountain-path, Seek still His com-pan-y.
3. Thy first trans-ac-tion be With God Himself a-bove; So shall thy busi-ness pros-per well, And all the day be love.

Copyright, 1894, by Frank Miller.

Come to Jesus.

1. Come to Je-sus, Come to Je-sus, Come to Je-sus just now; Just now come to Je-sus, Come to Je-sus just now.

2 He will save you,
3 Oh, believe Him.
4 He is able.
5 He is willing.
6 He'll receive you.
7 Call upon Him.
8 He will hear you.
9 Look unto Him.
10 He'll forgive you.
11 Flee to Jesus.
12 Only trust Him.
13 Jesus loves you.
14 Don't reject Him.
15 I believe Him.
16 He will bless you.
17 He will cleanse you.
18 He will clothe you.
19 Hallelujah, Amen.

"SONGS OF THE PEACEMAKER," COMPLETE.

WE confidently believe that this enlarged and revised edition of "SONGS OF THE PEACEMAKER" cannot be improved upon. It contains the choicest of words and music, both old and new. Selections suitable and in great abundance, for all kinds of Christian work and worship.

LIST OF COMPOSERS AND CONTRIBUTORS.

Dr. H. R. PALMER.
WM. J. KIRKPATRICK.
JNO. R. SWENEY.
E. O. EXCELL.
J. M. WHYTE.
CHAS. H. GABRIEL.
A. BIERLY.
J. G. DAILEY.
W. A. OGDEN.
J. H. KURZENKNABE.
FRANK M. DAVIS.
J. H. TENNEY.
A. J. SHOWALTER.
J. H. FILLMORE.
J. M. BLACK.
A. F. MYERS.
J. H. HALL.
GEO. C HUGG.
I. H. MEREDITH.
J. H. ALLEMAN.
GRANT C. TULLAR.
J. H. ROSECRANS.
TALLIE MORGAN.
P. KEIL, Jr.
GEO. A. MINOR.
S. C. FOSTER.
WILL L. THOMPSON.
Mrs. M. E. WILLSON.
Miss M. E. UPHAM.
Mrs. GRACE WEISER DAVIS.
Miss KATE O. CURTS.
Mrs. JOSEPH F. KNAPP.
Mrs. CLARA H. SCOTT.
C. F. PRICE.
J. G. FOOTE.
GEO. F. ROSCHE.
E. E. NICKERSON.
A. J. BUCHANAN.
J. W. WARD.
M. A. LEE.
Col. H. H. HADLEY.
GEO. N ROCKWELL.
HERBERT D. LOTHROP.
W. C. WEEDEN.
F. J. ST. CLAIR.
FRANK MILLER.
CHAS. EDW. PRIOR.
W. S. NICKLE.
S. M. BIXBY.
CARYL FLORIO.
IRA ORWIG HOFFMAN.
W. G. TOMER.
GRACE I. FOSTER.
FRED A. FILLMORE.
JAS. H. ROBINSON.
J. E. GLINES.

JOHN FOOTE.
S. J. VAIL.
WILLIAM A. GALPIN.
J. KINKLE.
LOWELL MASON.
W. H. MONK.
F. GIARDINI.
C. G. GLASER.
L. PLEYEL.
J. J. HUSBAND.
F. J. HAYDN.
G. F. HANDEL.
LEWIS EDSON.
J. J. ROSSEAU.
I. CONKEY.
C. H. A. MALAN.
W. TANSUR.
Rev. W. W. BENTLEY.
Rev. E. S. UFFORD.
Rev. R. LOWRY.
Rev. E. A. HOFFMAN.
Rev. E. F. MILLER.
Rev. J. H. WELCH.
Rev. I. BALTZELL.
Rev. J. M. DRIVER.
Rev. J. E SPILLMAN.
Rev. W. S. NICKLE.
Rev. O. E. MURRAY.
Rev. F. W. WARE.
Rev. J. E. RANKIN.
Rev. W. G. COOPER.
Rev. W. A. WILLIAMS.
Rev. H. N. LINCOLN.
Rev. A J. GORDON.
Rev. T. C. O'KANE.
Rev. C. C. MCCABE.
Rev. D. E. DORTCH.
Rev. A. C. FERGUSON.
Rev. W. A. SPENCER.
Rev. C. W. RAY.
Rev. R. M. MCINTOSH.
Rev. E. S. LORENZ.
Rev. JOSHUA GILL.
Rev. GEORGE COLES.
Rev. THOS. HASTINGS.
Rev. JOHN B. DYKES.
Dr. ARNE.
THE LINCOLN SHOWALTER CO.
THE R. M. MCINTOSH CO.
THE HOFFMAN MUSIC CO.
THE FOOTE BROTHERS.
THE MCDONALD-GILL CO.
THE EVANGELICAL PUBLISHING CO.
THE FILLMORE BROS.
R. R. MCCABE & CO.
W. P. DUNN & CO.

To the many eminent composers and publishers, the names of whom are given above, and whose contributions help to make this book what it is, we extend our sincere thanks.

W. S. WEEDEN, *Singing Evangelist,*
117 East 82d St., NEW YORK.

GEO. BEAVERSON,
15 Vandewater St., NEW YORK.

LEONARD WEAVER, *Evangelist,*
GRIMSBY, CANADA.

J. W. VAN DE VENTER,
805 Lewis Block, PITTSBURG, PA.

SONGS

OF THE

PEACEMAKER

A COLLECTION OF SACRED SONGS AND HYMNS FOR USE IN ALL SERVICES OF THE CHURCH, SUNDAY-SCHOOL HOME CIRCLE AND ALL KINDS OF EVANGELISTIC WORK. :: :: ::

EDITED BY

W. S. WEEDEN, GEO. BEAVERSON,

AND

LEONARD WEAVER
(Evangelist).

PUBLISHED BY

J. W. VAN DE VENTER & CO.,

NEW YORK:
W. S. WEEDEN,
441 PEARL ST.

PITTSBURG, PA.:
J. W. VAN DE VENTER,
805 LEWIS BLOCK.

CANADA AGENCY:
LEONARD WEAVER,
GRIMSBY, · · · · · · ONTARIO.

Copyright, 1895, by J. W. VAN DE VENTER & CO.   Canada. Copyright, 1895, by LEONARD WEAVER & CO.

PREFACE.

No ONE can estimate the power of Christian song. Who will measure the influence of the hymns of apostolic times, the chants of Gregory, or the lyrics of Isaac Watts and Charles Wesley? In the great revivals of recent years gospel hymns have been hardly less potent than the preaching of the most effective evangelists. This new collection of Christian songs ought to find a hearty welcome. The authors have made their selections with the greatest care. Hail to "**Songs of The Peacemaker!**" The glad words of the angel ring in our ears as we open this book—"On earth peace." The name is a good one. All the songs in the collection center about and exalt the life and character of the "**Prince of Peacemakers.**" Book of song, go thou to tens of thousands, carrying thy message of peace.

WILLIAM H. CRAWFORD,
President Allegheny College.

MEADVILLE, PA.

Blessed *are* the *Peacemakers:* for they shall
be called the children of God.
MATT. V. 9

NOTICE.
The words and music of nearly every piece in this book are copyright property, and cannot be reprinted in any form whatever without the written permission of the owners.
THE PUBLISHERS

SONGS OF THE PEACEMAKER.

He's the Prince of Peacemakers.

Rev. F. W. WARE.   J. E. GLINES.

Moderato.

1. He hath spoken, "Be still," the Re - buk - er of seas; The command was for me, and my
2. He hath quicken'd my soul by a life from a-bove; It was done by the Spir - it, its
3. He's a wonder - ful Je - sus, this Sav - ior of mine; He's the great Son of God— a Re-
4. I will love Him, and serve Him from now till I die; For His love fills my heart, and His

p rall.   *cres.*

heart is at ease; He hath hush'd in - to si - lence the waves and the winds, By ap-
es - sence is love. He hath pardon'd and wash'd me as white as the snow, And my
-deem - er Di - vine. He's my Strength and my Wisdom, my Life and my Lord, And en-
beau - ty my eye. He's the fair - est and dear - est of all to my soul, And our

CHORUS. *faster. mf*

- ply - ing His blood and re - mov - ing my sins,
heart with His love does this moment o'er-flow.   He's the Prince of Peacemakers, all
- thron'd in my heart, to be loved and a - dored,
lives shall be one, while e - ter - ni - ties roll.

glo - ry to God, To re-deem me, and cleanse me, He shed His own blood; My a-

- doption is seal'd, I'm a child of the King, And for-ev-er and ev-er of Je-sus I'll sing.

Copyright, 1892, by Francis W. Ware.

The Bridegroom Cometh!

Words and Melody by LEONARD WEAVER, Evangelist. Arr. by G. B.

1. O brother, are you ready should the Bridegroom come? Are your lamps well trim'd and bright? For sure He will come, And the time will not be long; Are you read-y if He came to-night?
2. The trumpet will be sounded when the Bridegroom comes, And the grave yield up its prey, The dead shall a-rise And meet Him in the skies; Are you read-y for that glo-rious day?
3. It may be at the gloaming when the Bridegroom comes, Or the ris-ing of the sun, So we watch, work and pray, And go sing-ing on our way; To the faith-ful He will say "well done."

What a meeting it will be, When the Sav-ior we shall see, And as-cend-ing we shall meet Him in the sky; With Him we shall ev-er be, And from ev-'ry sin be free; Are you
All the loved ones we shall meet, And with rapture we shall greet, All the ransom'd who have journey'd on be-fore; What a song of praise we'll sing When we stand around our King; Are you
When the vic-to-ry is won We shall have a star-ry crown, And in wor-ship we shall cast it at His feet, Cry-ing, "Worthy is the Lamb To receive the song and psalm; Are you

CHORUS.

read-y for the midnight cry? }
read-y for the heav'nly shore? } Yes, I am ready, yes, I am ready,
read-y for that bliss complete? }
ready, ready,

1. Read-y for my Lord to come;
2. Read-y for the call, Come home!

Yes, I'm ready, O,

Copyright, 1895, by Leonard Weaver,

Salvation through the Blood.

To my friend Evangelist Leonard Weaver.

Arr. from the London Hymn Book.
W. S. WEEDEN.

1. Not all the gold of all the world And all its wealth combined,
Could give re-lief or com-fort yield, To one dis-tract-ed mind;
'Tis on-ly to the pre-cious blood Of Christ the soul can fly,
There on-ly can a sin-ner find A flow-ing full sup-ply.

2. Gold could not give the heart re-lief The mal-e-fac-tor craved
Ah! no; 'twas thro' the Christ of God, That dy-ing man was saved;
He looked to Him who bleed-ing hung, A vic-tim by his side.
He saw, he cried, he heard, he knew, His soul was sat-is-fied.

3. Sal-va-tion thro' the blood my song, Re-demp-tion all my theme;
I bask be-neath His bless-ed smile, And drink at life's full stream;
And in a lit-tle while I'll go, To dwell with Him a-bove
Where not a cloud will in-ter-cept The full-ness of His love

CHORUS.

O, joy-ful news, O, hap-py news, The pre-cious, pre-cious blood

Copyright, 1895, by W. S. Weeden.

3 And now the mighty deed is done,
　On the cross, yes, on the cross.
　The battle's fought, the victory's won,
　On the cross, yes, on the cross.
　The rocks do rend the mountains quake,
　While Jesus doth atonement make,
　While Jesus suffers for your sake,
　　On the cross, yes, on the cross.

4 Where'er I go I'll tell the story
　Of the cross, yes, of the cross.
　In nothing else my soul shall glory,
　Save the cross, yes, save the cross.
　Yes, this my constant theme shall be,
　Through time, and in eternity,
　That Jesus suffered death for me,
　　On the cross, yes, on the cross.

Sought and Found. Concluded.

His mer - cy fail - eth nev - er, His love en - dures for - ev - er; May neith-er sin or fol - ly My dear Re-deem - er grieve!
No pow'r on earth can harm me, Nor ev - er can a - larm me, For He is ev - er turn - ing My dark - ness in - to day.

Alas! and Did My Savior Bleed?

ISAAC WATTS. Cho. by L. W.   Arr. by G. B.

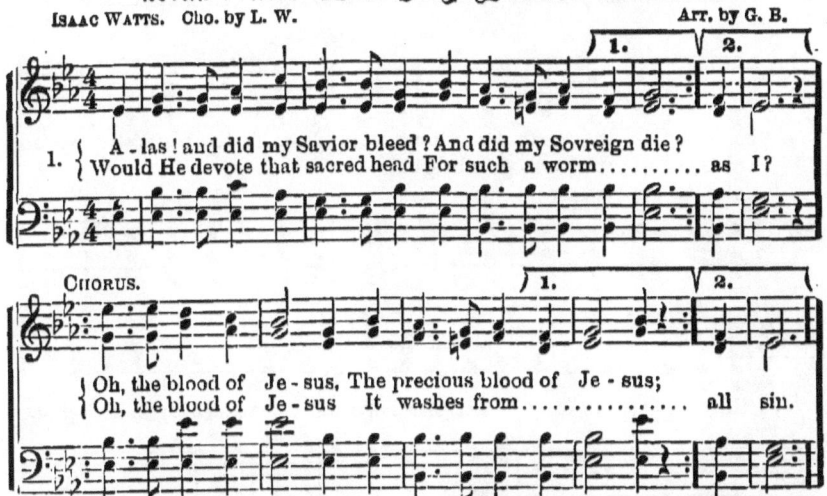

1. A - las! and did my Savior bleed? And did my Sovreign die?
   Would He devote that sacred head For such a worm......... as I?

CHORUS.

Oh, the blood of Je - sus, The precious blood of Je - sus;
Oh, the blood of Je - sus It washes from............ all sin.

2 Was it for crimes that I have done,
   He groaned upon the tree?
   Amazing pity! grace unknown!
   And love beyond degree!

3 Well might the sun in darkness hide,
   And shut his glories in,
   When Christ, the mighty Maker, died,
   For man the creature's sin.

4 Thus might I hide my blushing face
   While His dear cross appears;
   Dissolve my heart in thankfulness,
   And melt mine eyes to tears.

5 But drops of grief can ne'er repay
   The debt of love I owe;
   Here, Lord, I give myself away,—
   'Tis all that I can do.

Copyright, 1895, by Weeden and Weaver.

Do You Know the Song?

A. P. Cobb. J. H. Fillmore.

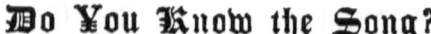

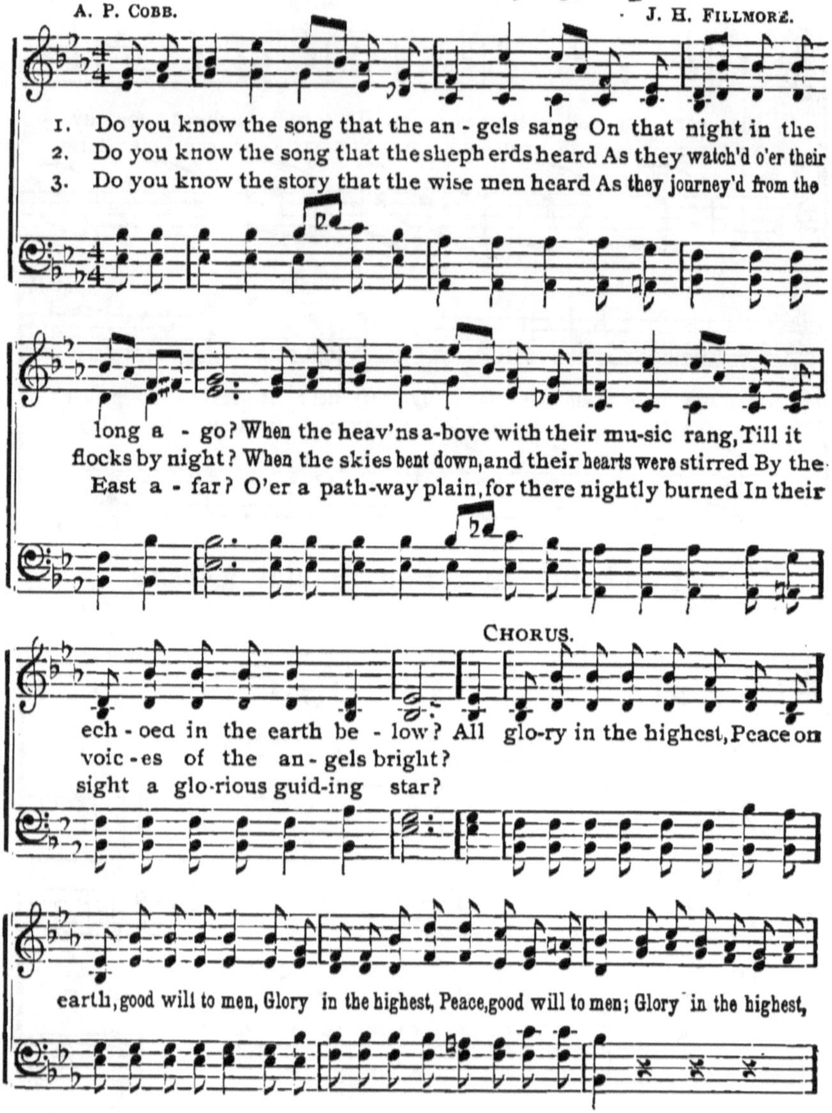

Wondrously Redeemed.

E. A. H.
Rev. Elisha A. Hoffman.

1. I have precious news to tell, hal-le-lu-jah! Christ has come with me to dwell, hal-le-lu-jah! By His grace and pow'r di-vine, He has chang'd this heart of mine, And He whispers, "I am thine," hal-le-lu-jah!
2. It was Christ's redemption blood, hal-le-lu-jah! That restored my soul to God, hal-le-lu-jah! He the cleansing stream applied, Flowing from His wounded side; I am saved and jus-ti-fied, hal-le-lu-jah!
3. I have found a precious friend, hal-le-lu-jah! On whose help I can de-pend, hal-le-lu-jah! Since He took my sins a-way, He has taught me how to pray, And to do His will each day, hal-le-lu-jah!

D.S. joic-ing night and day, As I walk the nar-row way, For He wash'd my sins a-way, hal-le-lu-jah!

Chorus.

Hal-le-lu — jah! I'm re-deemed! Oh, so won — drous-ly re-deemed!

Hal-le-lu-jah! I'm redeem'd! oh, hal-le-lu-jah! I'm redeem'd! Oh, so won-drous-ly redeem'd, yes, oh, so won-drous-ly redeem'd! I'm re-

Copyright, by The Hoffman Music Co.

Jesus Leads the Way.

Melody, "Auld Lang Syne."

Mrs. M. O. PAGE. Arr. by Mrs. CLARA H. SCOTT.

1. 'Tis sweet to lean on Je-sus's breast And know my sins for-giv'n,
2. And now my Je-sus leads the way, And I ac-cept-ance bring,
3. I'll tell the sto-ry o'er and o'er, It is so sweet to give,

'Tis sweet to think my earth-ly name Is writ-ten now in heav'n,
I stand with-in the noon-tide ray De-scend-ing from our King,
'Tis all the sto-ry that we need To teach us how to live;

'Tis sweet to think my jour-ney here Is all il-lumined by grace,
And this has made me strong to bear, And quick to do his will;
And all the sto-ry that we need To tell in heav'n a-bove,

D. S.—*'Tis sweet to think my jour-ney here Is all illumined by grace,*

D. S.

That I may nev-er feel a fear, For I shall see his face.
And watch-ing doth my heart pre-pare My mis-sion to ful-fill.
Is just the same old gos-pel theme Of Je-sus and his love;

That I may nev-er feel a fear, For I shall see his face.

By permission.   Copyright, 1894, by The Evangelical Publishing Co.

Be a Golden Sunbeam.

ISAAC NAYLOR.
CHAS. H. GABRIEL.

1. Be a gold-en sun-beam, ra-di-ant and bright, Chas-ing from life's pathway sor-row's frown-ing night; With thy gold-en sun-light dry the dew-y tear, Scat-ter from the sad heart all its doubt and fear.
2. When the way is gloom-y, cheer it with a song— Ban-ish mist and shad-ow as you march a-long; In the place of bri-ars strew the fairest flow'rs, Wreathing brows with roses pluck'd from heav'nly bowr's.
3. Be a gold-en sun-beam, bright, and pure, and fair, With thy smiles and son-nets light-en hu-man care; With the sweet-est mu-sic from the harp of love, Lure the sad and wea-ry to our home a-bove.

CHORUS.

Be a gold-en sun-beam, beau-ti-ful and bright, Scat-ter-ing clouds and dark-ness with thy shin-ing light:
Be a gold-en sun-beam, joy-ful-ly and glad Scat-ter-ing rays of sun-light (*Omit.*).............when the way is sad.

Copyright, 1894, by Chas. H. Gabriel. Used by per.

Bringing the World to Jesus. Concluded.

D.S. al Fine.

While it's called to-day, Glean-ing in the har-vest All a-long the way;

How They Crucified My Lord.
(JUBILEE SONG) Arr. by M. E. BLISS-WILLSON.

1. When I think how they cru-ci-fied my Lord, When I think how they cru-ci-fied my Lord, Oh, sometimes it causes me to tremble, tremble, tremble, When I think how they cru-ci-fied my Lord.

2. When I think how they crowned Him with the thorns.
3. When I think how they nailed Him to the tree.
4. When I think how they pierced Him in the side.
5. When I think how they laid Him in the tomb.
6. When I think how the stone was rolled away.
7. When I think how He rose up from the grave.

Used by permission.

Sweet Rose of Sharon.

Rev. F. W. WARE. By per.
J. E. GLINES.

SOLO OR DUET. *Lento.*

1. Rose of Sha - ron, Thy rich fragrance Fills the air where'er I roam,
2. Rose of Sha - ron, Great Physi - cian Of the mind and of the heart,
3. Rose of Sha - ron, my dear Shepherd, Feed the life in mer-cy giv'n,
4. Then, O Rose, sweet Rose of Sha - ron, Set me in the soil a - bove;
5. Let me grow, bless'd Rose of Sha - ron, As di - rect - ed by Thy love.

And the sweetness of Thy smil - ing Checks my tears and lifts my gloom.
Balm and bal-sam Thou hast brought me And I'm healed in ev - 'ry part.
Let me live and grow just like Thee Till I'm ripe and meet for heav'n,
Let me grow in Thy great gar - den, In the frost - less land of love.
Let me have thro' end-less a - ges, Fel - low - ship with Thee a - bove.

CHORUS. *Allegro moderato.* mf

Sweeter, dai - ly, Rose of Sha - ron, Grows the fra - grance of Thy name.

Onward, dai - ly, My dear Sav-ior, Moves the splen - dor of Thy fame.

Copyright, 1893, by Francis W. Ware.

Bringing in the Sheaves.

"The harvest is the end of the world."—Matt. 13, 39.

Words from "Songs of Glory."   Geo. A. Minor.

1. Sow-ing in the morn-ing, sow-ing seeds of kind-ness,
Sow-ing in the noon-tide and the dew-y eves; Waiting for the har-vest, and the time of reap-ing, We shall come re-joic-ing, bringing in the sheaves.

2. Sow-ing in the sun-shine, sow-ing in the shad-ows,
Fearing neither clouds nor winter's chilling breeze; By and by the har-vest, and the la-bor end-ed, We shall come re-joic-ing, bringing in the sheaves.

3. Go, then, ev-en weep-ing, sow-ing for the Mas-ter,
Tho' the loss sustain'd our spir-it oft-en grieves; When our weeping's o-ver, He will bid us wel-come, We shall come re-joic-ing, bringing in the sheaves.

Chorus.

Bring-ing in the sheaves, Bring-ing in the sheaves,
Bring-ing in the sheaves, Bring-ing in the sheaves.

1. We shall come re-joic-ing, bringing in the sheaves,
2. We shall come re-joic - - (*Omit*) - - ing, bringing in the sheaves.

From "Gospel Echoes," by per.

6 The worldling seeks for pleasure,
  In earthly vanity;
My treasures are in heaven,
  And that's enough for me.
Cho.—And that's enough for me,
    Enough of joy for me;
  My treasures are in heaven,
    And that's enough for me.

7 When ends our toil and sorrow,
  A better home I'll see,
And be with Christ forever,
  And that's enough for me.
Cho.—And that's enough for me,
    Enough of joy for me;
  To be with Christ forever,
    Oh, that's enough for me!

Copyright, 1878, 1887, 1893 by THE HOFFMAN MUSIC CO., Cleveland.

I Have Found Jesus.

Words and Melody furnished by Evangelist LEONARD WEAVER. Arr. by G. B.

1. I'm a pil-grim bound for glo-ry, I'm a pil-grim go-ing home;
2. Shall I tell you what induced me For the bet-ter land to start?
3. When I first commenc'd my jour-ney Ma-ny said, He'll turn a-gain;
4. When I reach the crys-tal riv-er I shall lay my ar-mor down
5. In His pres-ence I'll a-dore Him, Sing His prais-es o'er and o'er;

Come and hear me tell my sto-ry; All who love the Sav-ior, come.
'Twas the Sav-ior's lov-ing kind-ness O-ver-came and won my heart.
But they all were dis-ap-point-ed, For thro' grace I still re-main.
At the feet of my dear Sav-ior, And of Him re-ceive a crown.
I will walk a-bout the cit-y, Shouting glo-ry ev-er-more!

CHORUS.

I have found Jesus; He has redeemed me; O, how His glo-ry fills my soul!

Repeat pp

For at the foun-tain I have been drinking, And His Spir-it makes me whole.

Copyright, 1895, Weeden and Weaver.

Where He Leads I'll Follow. 39

"Come unto me, all ye that labor and are heavy-laden, and I will give you rest." Matt. 11: 28.

W. A. O.
W. A. OGDEN.

1. Sweet are the prom-is-es, Kind is the word; Dear-er far than
2. Sweet is the ten-der love Je-sus hath shown; Sweeter far than
3. List to His loving words, "Come un-to Me;" Wea-ry, heav-y-

an-y mes-sage man ev-er heard, Pure was the mind of Christ,
an-y love that mor-tals have known, Kind to the err-ing one,
lad-en, there is sweet rest for thee, Trust in His prom-is-es,

Sin-less I see; He the great ex-am-ple is, and pat-tern for me.
Faithful is He; He the great ex-am-ple is, and pat-tern for me.
Faithful and sure; Lean up-on the Sav-ior, and thy soul is se-cure.

CHORUS.

Where............ He leads I'll fol - low
Where He leads I'll fol-low, Where He leads I'll fol-low,

1.
Fol - - - low all the way.
Follow all the way, yes, follow all the way.

2.
Follow Jesus ev'ry day.

Copyright, 1885, by W. A. Ogden.

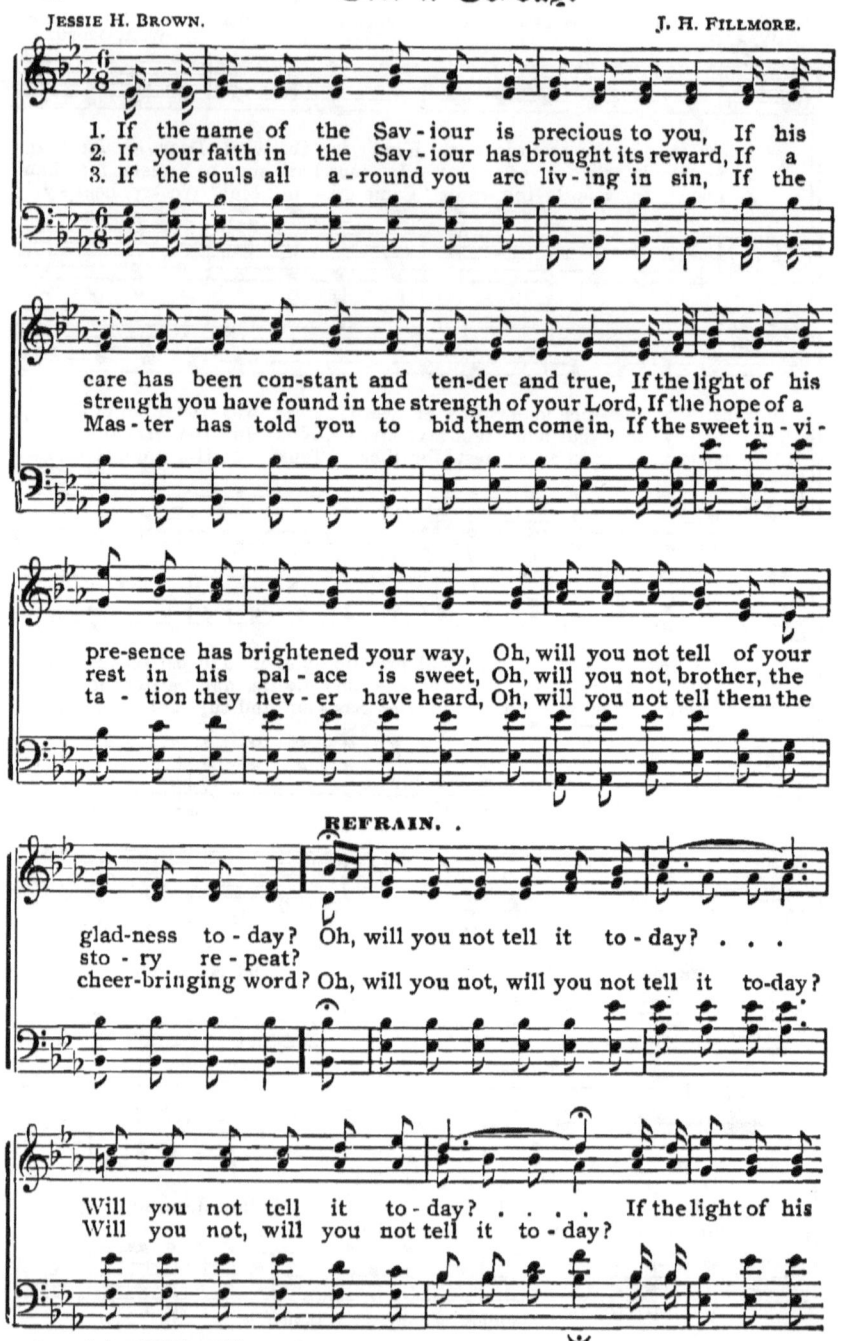

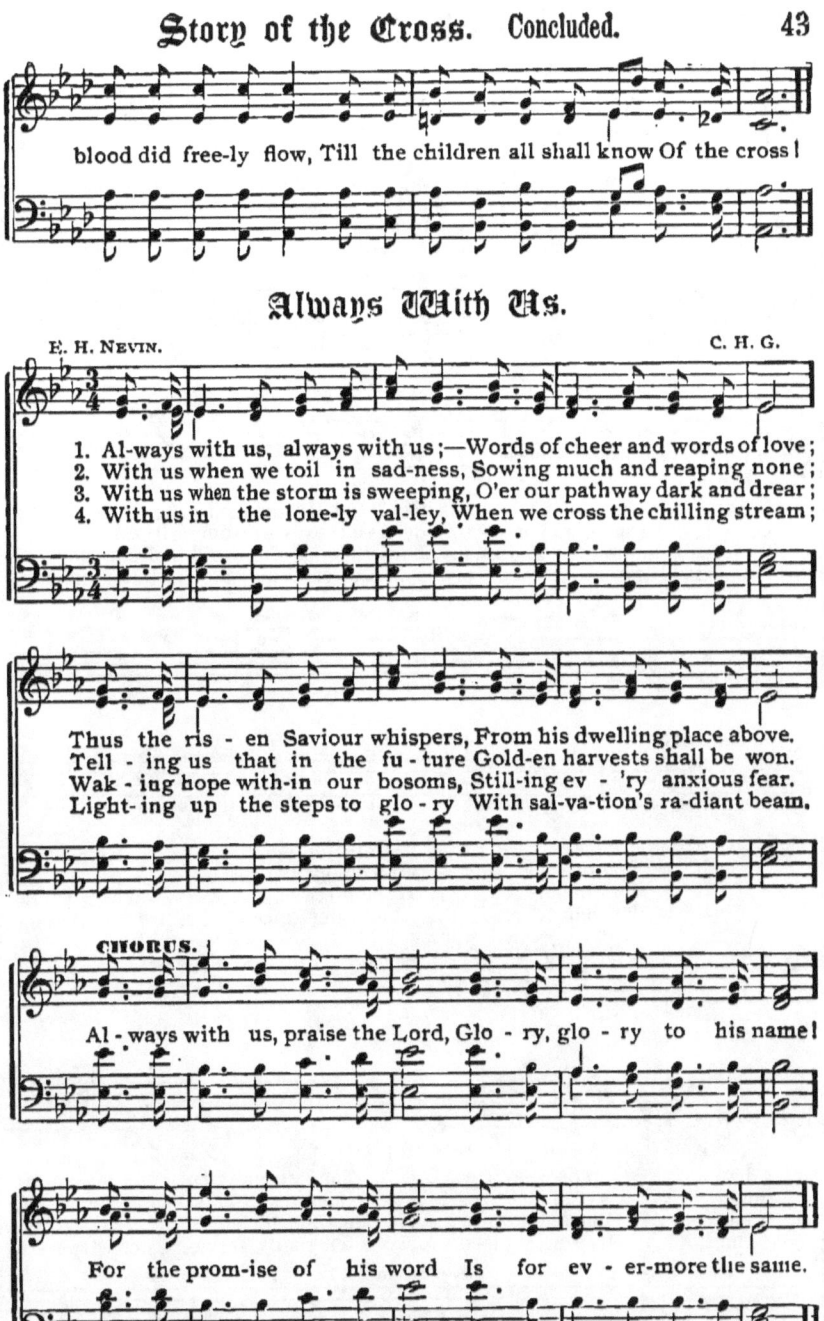

Saved by His Blood. Concluded.

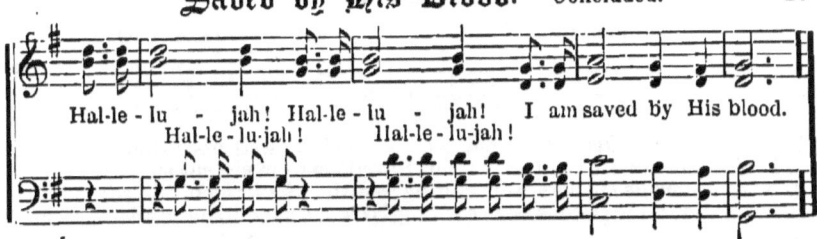

Wash My Sins Away.

Words and Music by Rev. E. S. UFFORD.

1. I once was on the road to woe, Wash my sins a-way,
2. I made the choice and en-tered in, Wash my sins a-way,
3. The Lord will give the hum-ble grace, Wash my sins a-way,
4. I mean to wrestle and en-dure, Wash my sins a-way,

I turned be-fore I sank too low, Wash my sins a-way.
I left be-hind my load of sin, Wash my sins a-way.
And lead them to the high-est place, Wash my sins a-way.
And make my own sal-va-tion sure, Wash my sins a-way.

REFRAIN.

'Twas a hap-py day when Je-sus wash'd, Wash'd my sins, sins a-way, O, hap-py day when Je-sus wash'd, Wash'd my sins a-way.

Copyright, 1895, by E. S. Ufford.

Precious Truth. Concluded.

hap - py cho-rus, Sing - ing, sing - ing, Our Savior's praise;
still the cho-rus, Tell - ing, tell - ing, His wondrous love;
-loud the cho-rus, Glo - ry, glo - ry, To God on high.

Singing, singing, singing, singing,
Tell-ing, tell-ing, tell-ing, tell-ing,
Glo-ry, glo-ry, glo-ry, glo-ry,

Jesus is Calling Now.

Rev. E. A. Hoffman. Geo. Beaverson.

1. Je - sus is call - ing you now! Come to His arms of love; He will pre-
2. Je - sus is call - ing to - day,— Why will you long-er wait? Cast all your
3. Je - sus is call - ing to you; Pledge Him, in solemn vow, Spir - it, and

CHORUS.

-pare your soul For the home a - bove }
sins a - way,— En - ter Mer-cy's gate. } Call-ing now, call-ing now,
life, and all,— He will save you now! }

Je-sus is call - ing now! At the cross hum-bly bow,—He will save you now!

Copyright, 1882, by John J. Hood.

3.
Now my heart is full of song,
Hallelujahs thrill my tongue,
 For His love and His goodness I know;
How can I but praise His name,
And His matchless love proclaim, [snow.
 Who has washed me as white as the

4.
Brother, burdened with your sin,
Do you long for peace within?
 Come to Jesus, your Savior and friend;
Unto Him your sins confess,
He will pardon, save, and bless,
 And of sorrow and sin make an end.

Copyright, 1894, by The Hoffman Music Co., Cleveland.

I'm Not Afraid.

H. H. HALL. GEO. BEAVERSON.

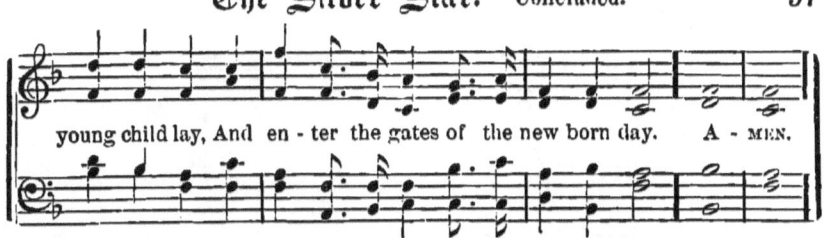

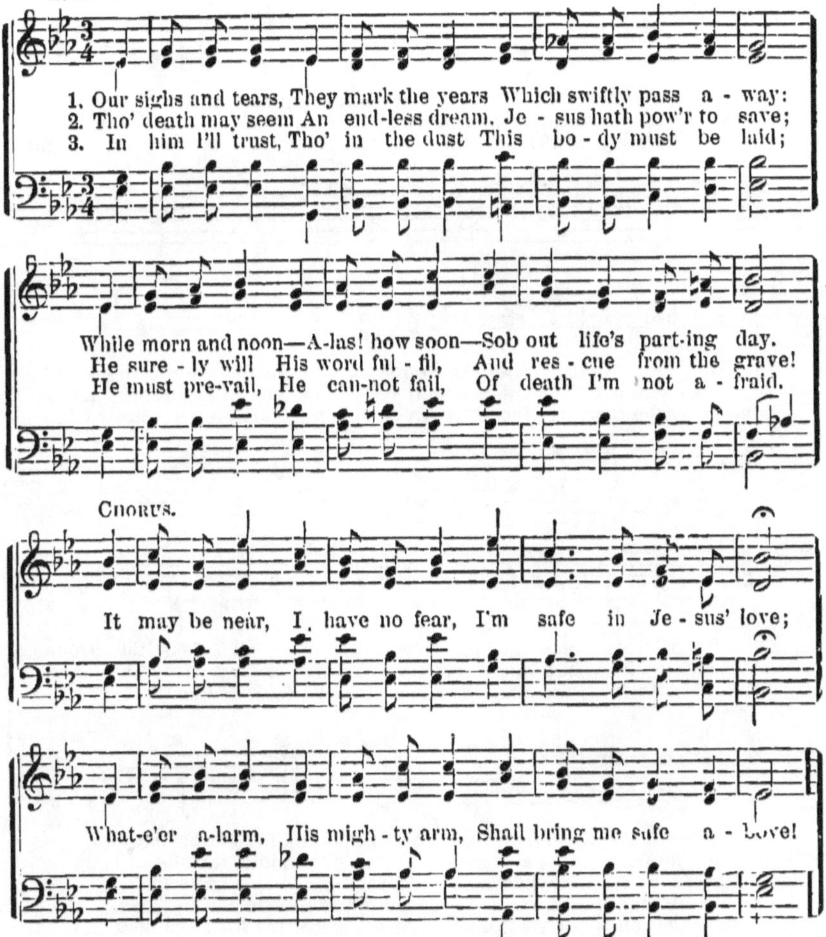

58. Little Things.

C. H. PAYNE, D.D., LL.D.   W. S. WEEDEN.

1. When you see a might-y for-est, With its tall and stur-dy trees,
2. When you gaze up-on a mountain, With its proud, ma-jes-tic form
3. When you see a state-ly tem-ple, Fair and beau-ti-ful and bright,

Lift-ing up their gi-ant branches; Wrestling with the win-try breeze;
Tow'ring up-ward to the heav-ens, All un-shak-en by the storm,
With its loft-y tow'rs and tur-rets Glist'ning in the sun's clear light,

Do not fail to learn the les-son Which the moaning winds re-sound,
Then re-mem-ber that the mountain Is built up of grains of sand,
Think how soon the no-ble structure Would to shapeless ru-in fall,

Ev-'ry oak was once an a-corn, All un-no-ticed on the ground.
Which an in-fant child might scat-ter With its ti-ny, fee-ble hand.
Were it not for sure foun-da-tions Firm-ly laid be-neath it all.

4 When you see a goodly nation
   Strong and free and proud and great,
With its statesmen, scholars, poets,
   All its men of high estate,
Keep in mind that all these great ones,
   To whom honors high you pay,
Once were only little people,
   Children such as we to-day.

5 In the building of our temple,
   Noble temple of the state,
As a refuge of true freemen,
   Both the lowly and the great,
Do not slight the little builders,
   Let us have some humble place,
Lay with us the sure foundation,
   Then you'll shout the capstone's grace.

Copyright, 1894, by W. S. Weeden.

62. Triumph By-and-By.

Dr. C. R. BLACKALL. H. R. PALMER.

1. The prize is set be-fore us, To win, his words implore us, The eye of God is o'er us, From on high, from on high; His loving tones are calling, While sin is dark, appalling; 'Tis Je-sus gently calling, He is nigh, he is nigh.
2. We'll fol-low where he lead-eth, We'll pasture where he feed-eth, We'll yield to him who pleadeth, From on high, from on high; Then naught from him shall sever, Our hope shall brighten ever, And faith shall fail us never, He is nigh, he is nigh.
3. Our home is bright a-bove us, No tri-als dark to move us, But Je-sus, dear, to love us, There on high, there on high; We'll give him best endeavor, And praise his name forever; His precious ones can never, Never die, never die.

CHORUS.

By and by we shall meet him, By and by we shall greet him, And with Jesus reign in glory, By and by, by and by; Jesus reign in glory, By and by.

BY PERMISSION.

5 Ring out, ring on, ye bells of trust,
For God hath said perform He must;
'Tis on His truth my all I stake,
No tempest-storms that Rock can shake.

6 Ring out, ring on, ye bells of heaven,
'Tis sweet to know all sin forgiven;
But oh, thy courts I soon shall see,
And share thy full felicity.

What a Gath'ring that will be.

J. H. K.   "Gather my saints together unto me."—Ps. 1. 5.   J. H. KURZENKNABE.

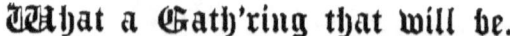

1. At the sounding of the trumpet, when the saints are gather'd home,
2. When the an-gel of the Lord proclaims that time shall be no more,
3. At the great and fi-nal judgment, when the hid-den comes to light,
4. When the gold-en harps are sounding, and the an-gel bands proclaim,

We will greet each oth-er by the crys-tal sea, crys-tal sea;
We shall gath-er, and the saved and ran-som'd see, ransom'd see,
When the Lord in all His glo-ry we shall see; we shall see;
In tri-umph-ant strains the glo-rious ju-bi-lee, ju-bi-lee;

With the friends and all the lov'd ones there a-wait-ing us to come,
Then to meet a-gain to-geth-er, on the bright ce-les-tial shore,
At the bid-ding of our Sav-ior, "Come, ye bless-ed, to my right,"
Then to meet and join to sing the song of Mo-ses and the Lamb,

CHORUS.

What a gath-'ring of the faith-ful that will be! What a gath - -
What a gath'ring of the
-'ring, gath - - 'ring At the sounding of the
loved ones when we'll meet with one an-oth-er.

By per. of J. H. Kurzenknabe, owner of copyright.

What a Gath'ring. Concluded.

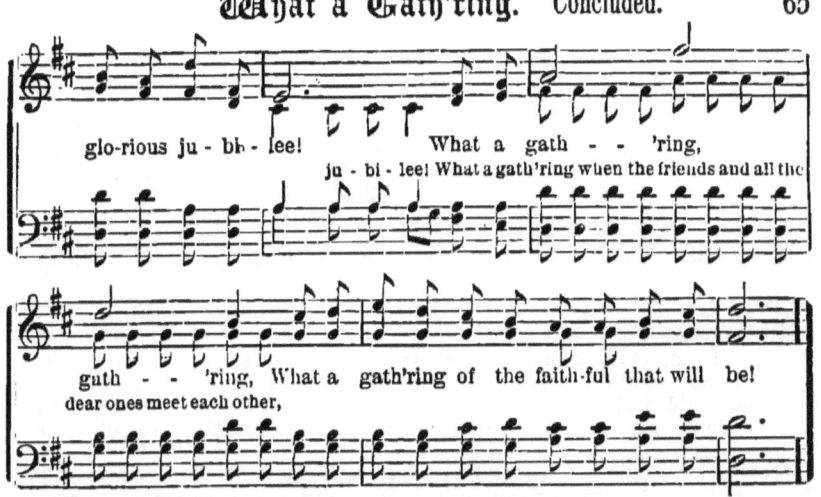

Nothing but the Blood of Jesus.

R. L.   R. LOWRY.

1. What can wash a-way my sin? Nothing but the blood of Jesus;
   What can make me whole a-gain? Nothing but the blood of Jesus.
2. For my cleansing this I see—Nothing but the blood of Jesus;
   For my pardon this my plea—Nothing but the blood of Jesus.

CHORUS.
Oh, precious is the flow That makes me white as snow;
No other fount I know, Nothing but the blood of Jesus.

3 Nothing can for sin atone,
   Nothing but the blood of Jesus;
 Naught of good that I have done,
   Nothing but the blood of Jesus.

4 This is all my hope and peace—
   Nothing but the blood of Jesus;
 This is all my righteousness—
   Nothing but the blood of Jesus.

Copyright, 1876, by Robert Lowry. Used by per.

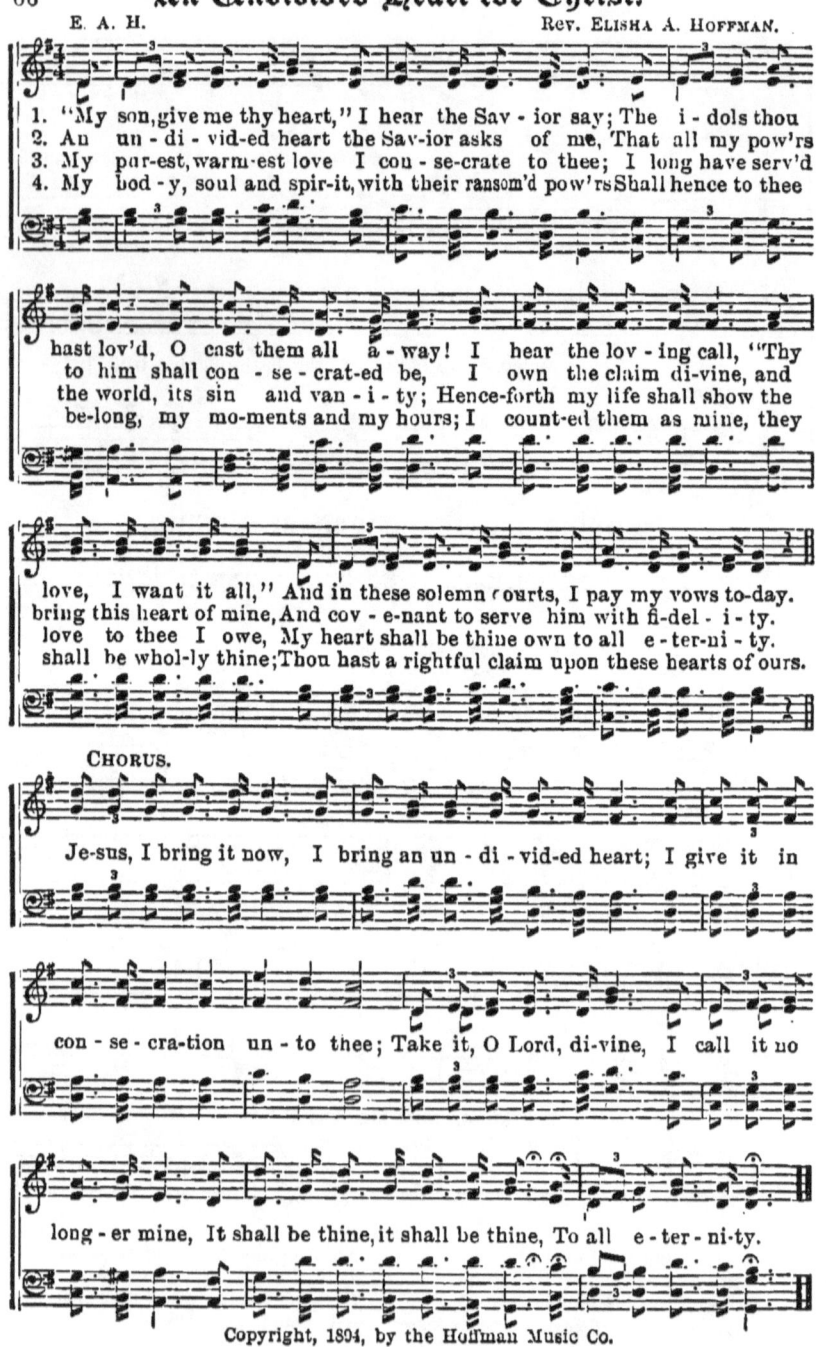

He Saves to the Uttermost.

73

FANNY J. CROSBY. CARYL FLORIO.

1. Our bless-ed Re-deem-er came down from a-bove To bring us good tid-ings of won-der-ful love; Then list-en with gladness, His message re-ceive:—He saves to the ut-termost all who be-lieve.
2. Be-hold, He is call-ing! No long-er de-lay; His arms are extend-ed in mer-cy to-day; He waits to be gracious, your souls to re-ceive:—He saves to the ut-termost all who be-lieve.
3. Come hith-er, ye thirst-y, wher-e'er you may be, Life's wa-ters are flow-ing, sal-va-tion is free; O come with-out mon-ey, full par-don re-ceive:—He saves to the ut-termost all who be-lieve.
4. O come to the ban-quet pre-pared for the world, And rest 'neath His standard so wide-ly un-furl'd; There's room, and the welcome that all may re-ceive:—He saves to the ut-termost all who be-lieve.

REFRAIN.

He saves to the ut-ter-most, Saves to the ut-ter-most, Saves to the ut-ter-most All who be-lieve.

Copyright, 1894, by S. M. Bixby. Used by permission.

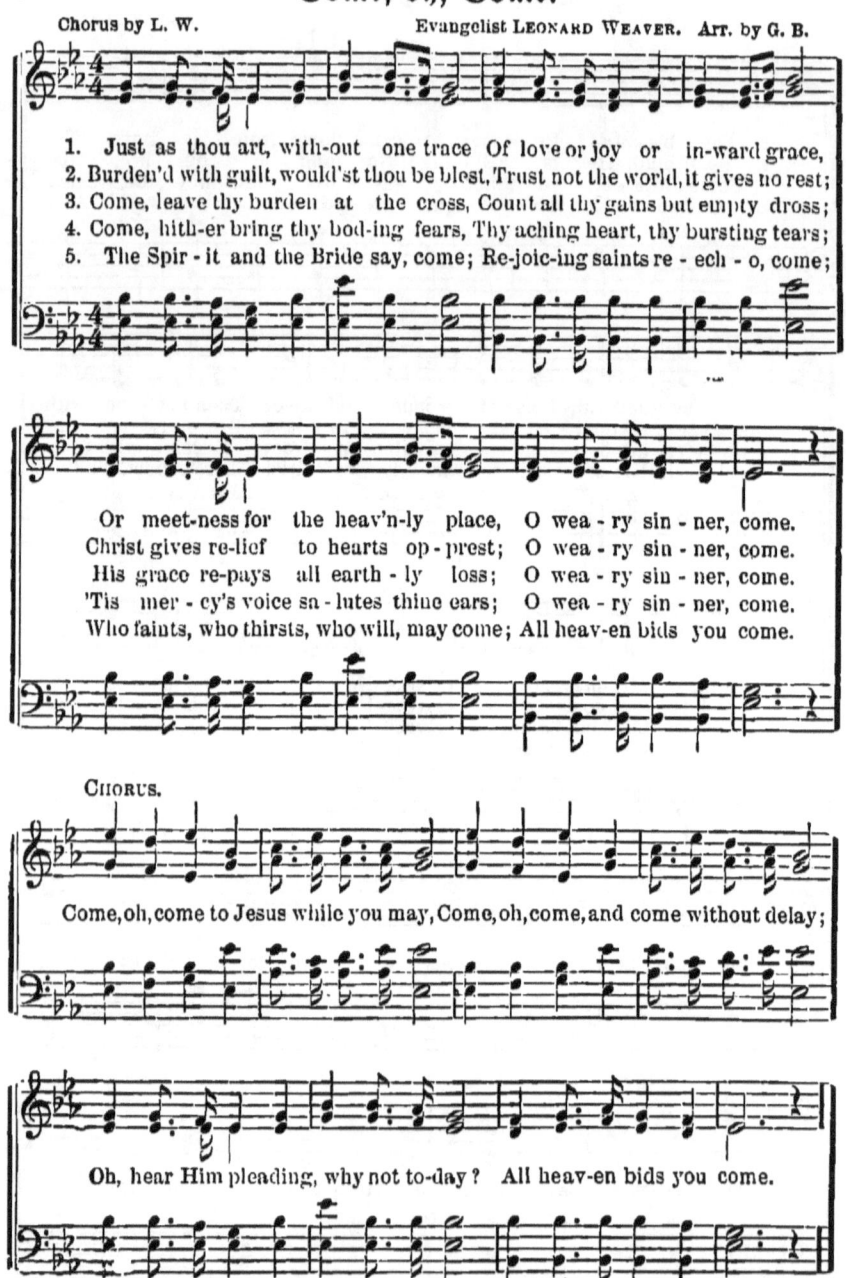

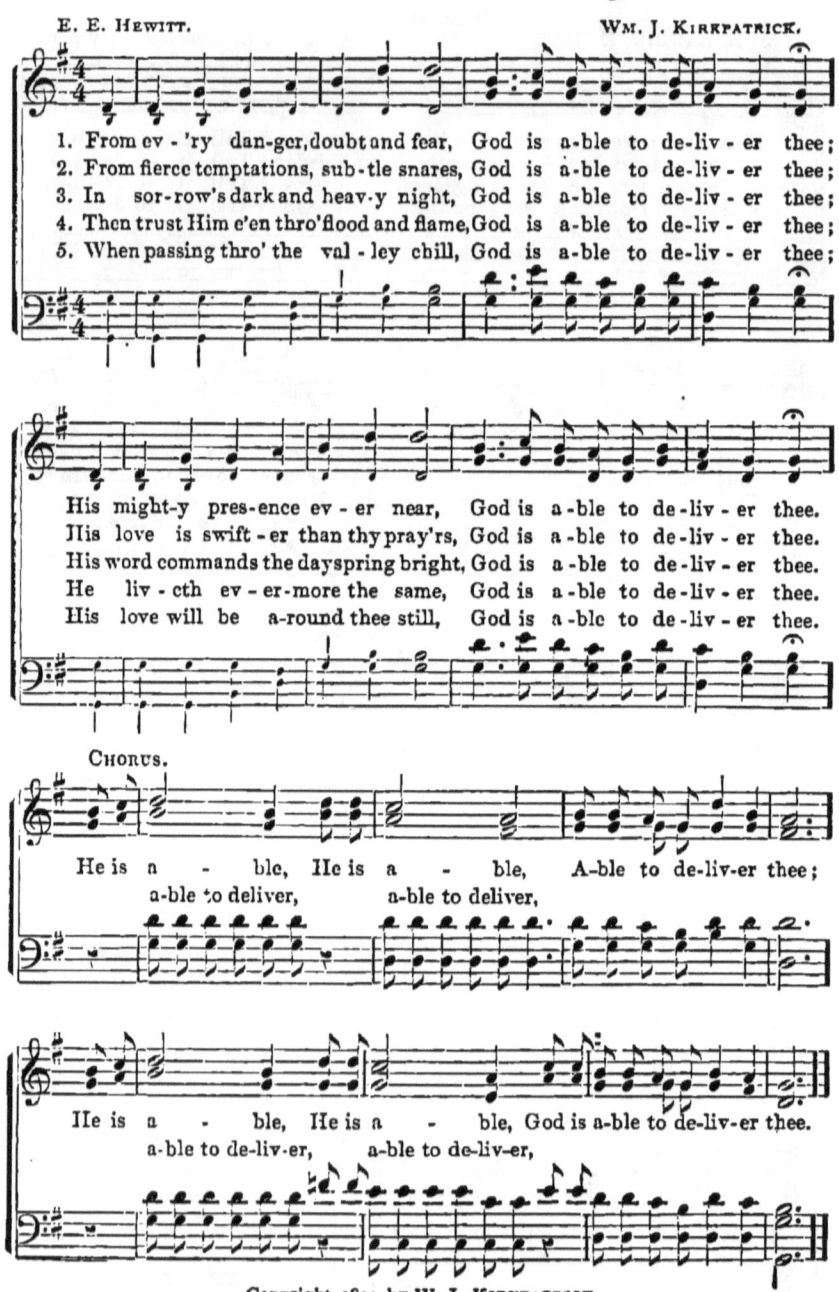

Christ Victorious.

77

EVALYN COUARD, Deaconess, New York City.
KATE O. CURTS, Deaconess, New York City.

Moderato.

1. Walking dai - ly with the Master, List'ning hour - ly to His voice;
2. Lift-ing bur - dens for our neighbors That are great - er than our own,
3. Trusting quiet - ly in as-sur-ance That our Mas - ter doth partake

Helping Him.. His sheaves to gather—In His work.. our hearts rejoice.
Helping those.. who faint around us To ap - proach the roy-al throne.
Of our tri - als and our triumphs; We shall win... for "Jesus' sake."

CHORUS.
Marcato.

Christ vic - to-rious! oh, the glo - ry Of the glad tri-umph-ant song—

When the na-tions learn the sto - ry And to Je - sus Christ be - long.

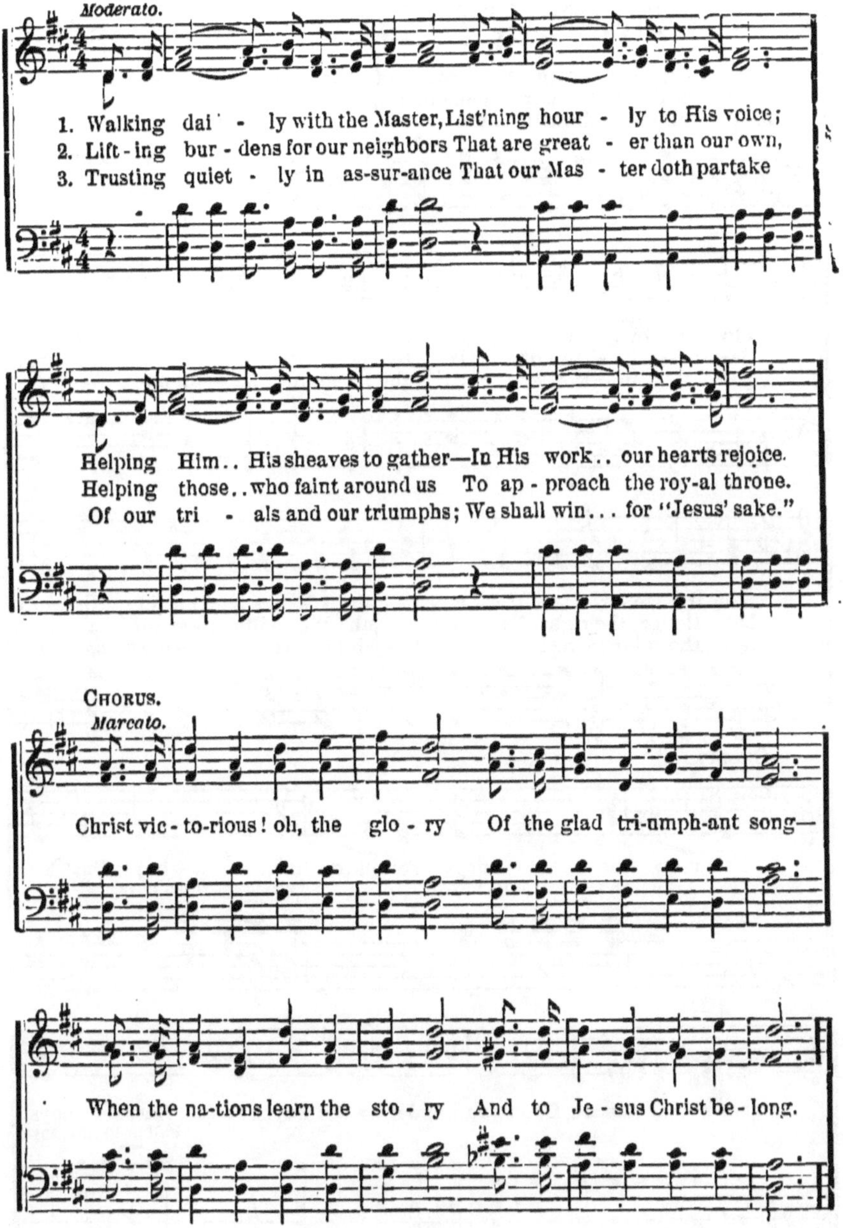

Copyright, 1894, by W. S. Weeden.

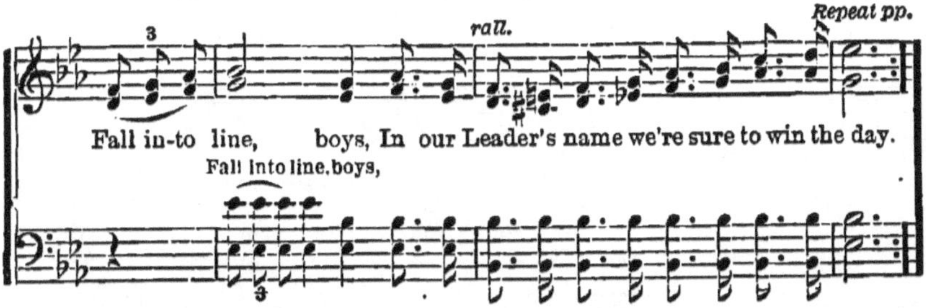

Fall into Line, Boys. Concluded.

Fall in-to line, boys, In our Leader's name we're sure to win the day.
Fall into line, boys,

Step Out on the Promise.

From "The Highway." Arr. by E. F. M. E. F. MILLER. By per.

1. O mourn-er in Zi-on, how bless-ed art thou, For Je-sus is wait-ing to com-fort thee now, Fear not to re-ly on the word of thy God; Step out on the promise,—get un-der the blood.
2. O ye that are hun-gry and thirst-y, re-joice! For ye shall be filled; do you hear that sweet voice In-vit-ing you now to the ban-quet of God? Step out on the promise,—get un-der the blood.
3. Who sighs for a heart from in-iq-ui-ty free? O, poor troubled soul! there's a prom-ise for thee, There's rest, wea-ry one, in the bos-om of God; Step out on the promise,—get un-der the blood.
4. Step out on this prom-ise, and Christ thou shalt win, "The blood of His Son cleanseth us from all sin," It cleans-eth me now, hal-le-lu-jah to God; I rest on the promise,—I'm under the blood.

Copyright, 1884, by E. F. Miller.

82. The Pharisee and Publican.

LEONARD WEAVER, Evangelist. W. S. WEEDEN.

1. There went to the tem-ple to of-fer up prayer, A Pub-li-can and Phar-i-see bold: And you who are hop-ing by works to be saved, Pray, list to the sto-ry so old. The Phar-i-see stood and prayed with him-self And glo-ried in what he had done; As if by his mer-it he

2. The Pub-li-can stood and smote on his breast, Not dar-ing to look to the sky, For he felt his con-di-tion and owned with contrition, No mer-it had he to come nigh. Have mer-cy, O God! on a sin-ner like me, This alone was the cry of his heart; Whilst the Phar-i-see wondered why

3. The Pub-li-can's prayer for mer-cy was heard, He was blest and for-giv-en that day; Whilst he who came boasting received not the blessing, De-ceived he went emp-ty a-way. Then trust not your goodness to save you from sin, Plead on-ly God's mer-cy so free; And then you be-liev-ing, His

Copyright, 1894, by W. S. Weeden.

The Pharisee and Publican. Concluded.

thought to in-her-it A place in the heav'n-ly home.
God did not bid, The Pub-li-can sin-ner de-part.
fa-vor re-ceiv-ing, The glo-ries of heav'n shall see.

CHORUS.

It's not by my working, it's not by my praying, Sal-va-tion from sin can be won; It is by be-liev-ing, It is by re-ceiv-ing, I'm saved thro' faith in God's Son.

The Lord's Prayer.

Matt vi.   GREGORIAN.

1. Our Father, who art in heaven, | hallowed | be Thy | name; || Thy kingdom come, Thy will be done on | earth, : as it | is in | heaven:
2. Give us this | day our | daily | bread; || And forgive us our debts, as | we for- | give our | debtors.
3. And lead us not into temptation, but de- | liver | us from | evil; || For Thine is the kingdom, and the power, and the glory, for- | ever. | A- | men.

Waiting by the Open Door. Concluded.

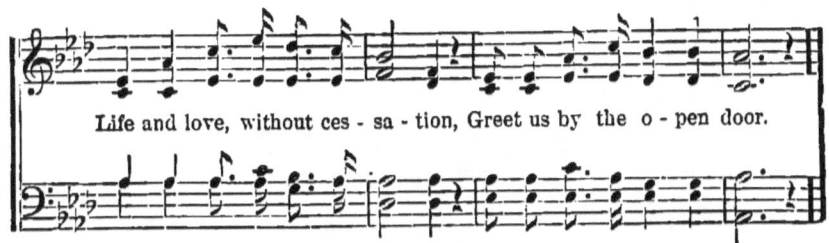

Life and love, without ces - sa - tion, Greet us by the o - pen door.

Amazing Grace.

NEWTON.   J. G. FCOTE.
Slow.

1. A - maz - ing grace! how sweet the sound, That sav'd a wretch like me,
2. 'Twas grace that taught my heart to fear, And grace my fears re-lieved;
3. Thro' ma - ny dan - gers, toils and snares I have al - read - y come;

I once was lost, but now am found, Was blind but now I see.
How pre - cious did that grace ap-pear, The hour I first be-lieved.
'Tis grace has brought me safe thus far, And grace will lead me home.

D. S.—Was sav'd by grace, am kept by grace, This theme my song shall be.

CHORUS.   *D. S.*

A - maz - ing grace! a - maz - ing grace, How sweet its sound to me,

* From "New Hymns, by per."

On Calvary There Stood a Cross.

Rev. ELISHA A. HOFFMAN. Rev. J. H. WELCH.

Slow.

1. On Cal-va-ry there stood a Cross, And nailed thereon was One
2. There the Re-deem-er gave His blood To ran-som me from sin,
3. Up-on that Cross, that bit-ter Cross, My weight of guilt He bore,
4. Be-fore that cross I weep and pray, And worship and a-dore,

Who was the bear-er of my sin, God's well-be-lov-ed Son.
And made an end of all my guilt, And brought redemption in.
Se-cured a clear-ance for my sins; My soul can ask no more.
And God's free grace I will ex-tol And laud for ev-er-more.

CHORUS.

Oh, the blood of the Lamb! Oh, the blood of the Lamb That was shed on Cal-va-ry! It was shed for you, it was shed for me, When He died up-on the tree.

Copyright, 1891, by the HOFFMAN MUSIC CO.

Wonderful Story of Love. Concluded.

Won - der - ful!
Won - der-ful sto - ry of love: won-der-ful sto - ry of love!

At the Cross I'll Abide.

I. B. "And many women were there."—Matt. 27 : 55. I. BALTZELL.

1. O Je - sus, Sav-ior, I long to rest Near the cross where Thou hast died:
2. My dy - ing Je - sus, my Savior God, Who hast borne my guilt and sin,
3. O Je-sus, Savior, now make me Thine, Nev-er let me stray from Thee;
4. The cleansing pow'r of Thy blood apply, All my guilt and sin re-move;

For there is hope for the aching breast, At the cross I will a - bide.
Now wash me, cleanse me with Thine own blood, Ev-er keep me pure and clean.
Oh, wash me, cleanse me, for Thou art mine, And Thy love is full and free.
Oh, help me, while at Thy cross I lie, Fill my soul with per-fect love.

CHORUS.

At the cross, I'll a - bide, At the cross, I'll a - bide,
At the cross, I'll abide, At the cross, I'll abide,

At the cross I'll abide, There His blood is applied; At the cross I am sanctified.

By permission.

Soldiers of the Lord. Concluded.

Nothing but Thy Blood.

Words arr. by J. W. Van De Venter. Music arr. by W. S. Weeden.

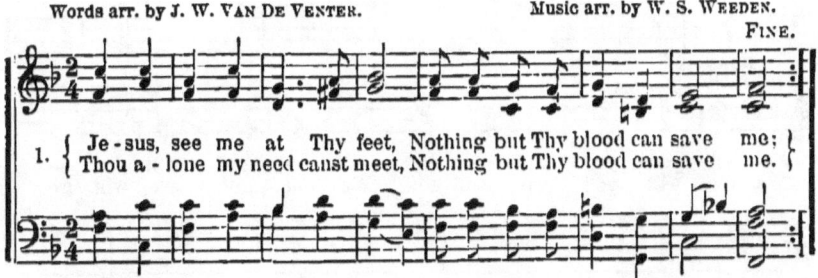

D.C.—To Thy cross, O Lamb of God, Nothing but Thy blood can save me.

2 See my heart, Lord, torn with grief,
  Precious Savior, send relief.

3 As I am, oh, hear me pray,
  I can come no other way.

4 All that I can do is vain,
  I can ne'er remove a stain.

5 Lord, I cast myself on Thee,
  From my guilt, oh, set me free.

Copyright, 1894, by W. S. Weeden.

4 Each saint has a mansion, prepared and all furnished,
Ere from his clay house he is summoned to move;
Its gates and its towers with glory are burnished.
Oh, say, will you go to the Eden above?

5 March on, happy pilgrims, the land is before you,
And soon its ten thousand delights we shall prove;
Yes, soon shall we walk o'er the hills of bright glory,
And drink the pure joys of the Eden above,

Copyright, 1895, by Weeden and Weaver.

Come Close to the Savior. Concluded.

Rockingham. L. M.

WM. COWPER.
LOWELL MASON.

1. What var-ious hin-dran-ces we meet In com-ing to the mer-cy seat! Yet who that knows the worth of pray'r, But wish-es to be oft-en there?
2. Pray'r makes the darken'd clouds withdraw; Pray'r climbs the ladder Ja-cob saw; Gives ex-er-cise to faith and love; Brings ev-ery bless-ing from a-bove.
3. Re-strain-ing pray'r, we cease to fight; Pray'r makes the Christian's armor bright; And Sa-tan trembles when he sees The weak-est saint up-on his knees.

4 Have you no words? Ah! think again;
Words flow apace when you complain,
And fill your fellow-creature's ear
With the sad tale of all your care,

5 Were half the breath thus vainly spent
To heaven in supplication sent,
Your cheerful song would oftener be,
"Hear what the Lord hath done for me!"

Onward Up the Highway. Concluded.

high-way, Let .... our voic-es ring ....
Let us make our hap-py voic-es ring, ev-er ring.

We Praise Thee, O Lord.

Rev. WM. APPEL.   A. BEIRLY.

1. We praise Thee, O Lord, For the smile of Thy face, For the health of Thy
2. We praise Thee, O Lord, For the light of Thy love, For the dew of Thy
3. We praise Thee, O Lord, For the strength of Thine arm, For Thy care and pro-
4. We praise Thee, O Lord, For Thy coming a-gain, For Thy glo-ri-ous

CHORUS.

sun-shine, The pow'r of Thy grace.
mer-cy That comes from a-bove.
-tec-tion That shields us from harm.
kingdom, Thy won-der-ful reign.

We praise Thee, dear Savior, A-gain and a-gain, We praise Thee, hal-le-lu-jah! for-ev-er a-men.

From "Golden Grain, No. 1," by per. of A. Beirly, publisher.

Come, Saints, and Adore Him. Concluded.

ceas- ing a - rise, And join the full cho- rus that gladdens the skies.

Yield not to Temptation.

Words and Music by H. R. PALMER.

1. Yield not to tempta-tion, For yielding is sin; Each vict'ry will help you
2. Shun e- vil companions; Bad language dis- dain; God's name hold in rev'rence,
3. To Him that o'ercometh God giv-eth a crown; Thro' faith we will conquer,

Some other to win. Fight manful- ly on-ward, Dark passions sub-due,
Nor take it in vain. Be thoughtful and earn-est, Kind-hearted and true,
Though often cast down. He who is our Saviour, Our strength will renew:

CHORUS.

Look ev- er to Je- sus, He'll car-ry you through, Ask the Saviour to help you,

Comfort, strengthen, and keep you, He is willing to aid you, He will carry you thro'.

By permission of Dr. H. R. PALMER, owner of Copyright.

Pass It On.

Rev. HENRY BURTON, A.M.   WM. J. KIRKPATRICK.

1. Have you had a kindness shown? Pass it on, pass it on! 'Twas not given for thee a-lone, Pass it on, pass it on! Let it trav-el down the years, Let it wipe an-oth-er's tears; Till in heav'n the deed appears,
2. Did you hear the lov-ing word! Pass it on, pass it on! Like the sing-ing of a bird? Pass it on, pass it on! Let its mu-sic live and grow, Let it cheer an-oth-er's woe; You have reaped what others sow,
3. Have you found the heav'nly light? Pass it on, pass it on! Souls are grop-ing in the night, Daylight gone, daylight gone! Hold your lighted lamp on high, Be a star in some one's sky, He may live who else would die,

D.S.—Christ, you live a-gain, Live for Him, with Him you reign,

FINE. CHORUS.

Pass it on, pass it on! Pass it on, Pass it on, pass it on! pass it on, Cheerful word or loving deed, Pass it on, pass it on, Live for self, you live in vain; Live for

D.S.

Copyright, 1888, by Wm. J. Kirkpatrick.

102. Cheer for the Thirsty.

C. W. R.
C. W. RAY.

SOLO OR SELECT VOICES.

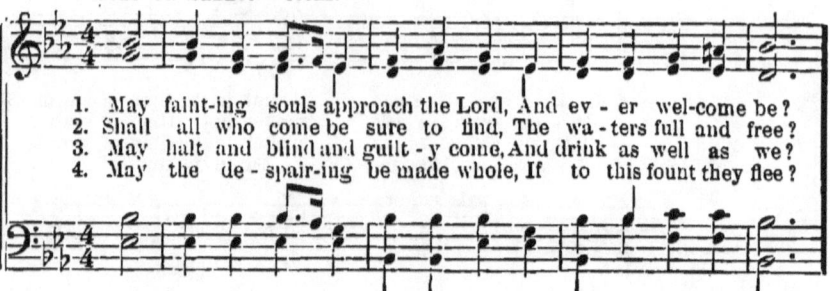

1. May faint-ing souls approach the Lord, And ev - er wel-come be?
2. Shall all who come be sure to find, The wa - ters full and free?
3. May halt and blind and guilt - y come, And drink as well as we?
4. May the de - spair-ing be made whole, If to this fount they flee?

CHORUS ECHO. *p* *pp* FULL CHORUS.

O can it be? Can it be? Trust-ing to the Sav-ior's word; O let them come and see! Come and see! Come and see!

ECHO. *p* *pp*

DUET. *After last stanza repeat with full chorus.*

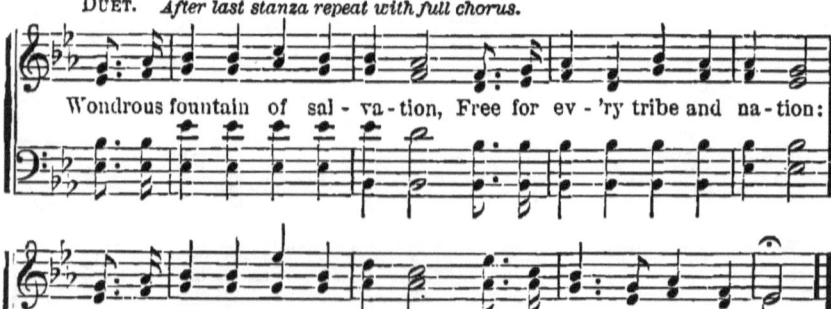

Wondrous fountain of sal - va - tion, Free for ev - 'ry tribe and na - tion: Free to all of ev - 'ry sta - tion, Fount of life for - ev - er free!

Copyright, 1894, by C. W. Ray.

My Spirit is Free.

W. A. S.
Rev. W. A. Spencer, D.D. By per.

1. I follow the footsteps of Jesus, my Lord, His Spirit doth lead me along; I walk in the pathway made plain by His word. And He fills all my soul with this song.
2. A leper He found me, polluted by sin, From which He alone can set free; He spake, in His mercy, "I will, be thou clean." And He instantly purified me.
3. A captive in woe to my prison of night, The Master hath open'd the door; Shout aloud of deliv'rance, ye angels of light. Praise His name, O my soul, evermore,
4. Proclaim it, 'tis done, full salvation is wrought For sinners from sorrow and woe; Sing aloud of His grace who my pardon has bought, For His blood washes whiter than snow.

Refrain.

Glory to God, my spirit is free, Glory to God, He purifies me; I'm walking the thorn path, but joyful I'll be While following Jesus my Lord.

104. Jesus Tenderly Calling.

"Come unto me, all ye that labor and are heavy-laden, and I will give you rest."—Matt. xi: 28.

J. G. FOOTE.   JOHN.

1. Je - sus is call - ing, ten-der-ly call - ing, Sin-ner, thy Sav - ior now pleads for thee; Stand-ing and knock-ing, anx - ious-ly wait - ing, Long-ing to save thee and set thee free.
2. Sin-ner, 'tis Je - sus, like the good Shepherd, Out on the des - ert to find His sheep; When He hath found it Heav-en re - joic - es; Sin - ner, thy Sav - ior can save and keep.
3. Prod-i - gal son, thy Fa-ther is wait - ing, Anxious and long-ing for thy re - turn; He will for-give thee, wel-come and bless thee, Glad-ly em-brace thee: then why not come?
4. Chiefest of sin - ners Je - sus will wel-come, Be of good cheer, He will say to thee; He will re-move your ev - 'ry transgres - sion, Blot-ting them out, and will set thee free.

D.S.—Will you not heed His ten - der en - treat - ies?
Why not re - ceive Him, His voice o - bey?

CHORUS.

Je - sus is call - ing, ten-der-ly call - ing, Sin-ner, He pleads, oh, hear Him to - day;

From "New Hymns," by per.

Trying to Shine for Jesus. Concluded.

pathway here be-low, Trying to shine for Je-sus wherev-er we go.

Blessed be the Name.

Words and Music arr. by Rev. O. E. Murray.

1. How sweet the name of Je-sus sounds, Blessed be the name of the Lord;
2. It makes the wounded spir-it whole, Blessed be the name of the Lord;
3. It soothes the troubled sinner's breast, Blessed be the name of the Lord;
4. Then will I tell to sin-ners round, Blessed be the name of the Lord;
5. There's music in the Savior's name, Blessed be the name of the Lord.

It soothes our sorrows, heals our wounds, Blessed be the name of the Lord.
'Tis man-na to the hun-gry soul, Blessed be the name of the Lord.
It gives the wea-ry sweet-est rest, Blessed be the name of the Lord.
What a dear Sav-ior I have found, Blessed be the name of the Lord.
Let ev-'ry heart His love proclaim, Blessed be the name of the Lord.

CHORUS.

Blessed be the name, blessed be the name, Blessed be the name of the Lord, the Lord.

Copyright, 1895, by O. E. Murray. By per.

112. Come Unto Me.

W. H. Ross.   C. F. Price. Arr. by G. B.

1. O list the voice of Jesus say, "Come unto Me, Come unto Me." It whispers to you ev'ry day, "Come unto Me, Come unto Me. I bore the cross on Calvary, I suffered shame and agony, I paid the debt to set you free, Come unto me, Come unto Me."

2. "Come, weary with earth's toils and care, Come unto Me, Come unto Me. Come, I with you my joy will share, Come unto Me, Come unto Me. Come, all your burdens lay aside, and trust in Me, whate'er betide, And I your steps will safely guide, Come unto me, Come unto Me."

3. "Come, ye who have no friends nor home, Come unto Me, Come unto Me. No longer friendless ye shall roam, Come unto Me, Come unto Me. And in My Father's house so blest, where all is joy, and peace, and rest, Come, lean upon Thy Savior's breast, Come unto me, Come unto Me."

4. "And ye who have both friends and gold, Come unto Me, Come unto Me. In Me, your Savior now behold. Come unto Me, Come unto Me. Ye can in no wise enter in, until you're cleansed from ev'ry sin. Come now, and plunge in Calvary's stream, Come unto me, Come unto Me."

Chorus.
Come unto Me, Come unto Me, Come unto Me, Come unto Me, All ye that

Copyright, 1895, by C. F. Price.

Come Unto Me. Concluded.

Jesus Saves Me Now.

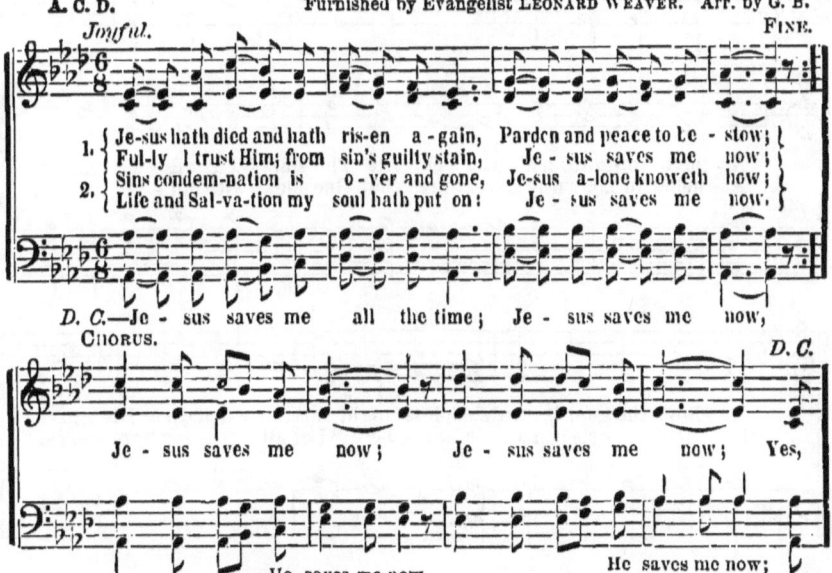

3 Satan may tempt, but he never shall reign,
  That Christ will never allow;
  Doubts I have buried, and this is my strain,
  "Jesus saves me now."

4 Resting in Jesus, abiding in Him,
  Gladly my faith can avow,—
  Never again need my pathway be dim:
  Jesus saves me now.

5 Jesus is stronger than Satan and sin,
  Satan to Jesus must bow;
  Therefore I triumph without and with-
  Jesus saves me now.   [in:

6 Sorrow and pain may beset me about,
  Nothing can darken my brow;
  Battl'ing in faith, I can joyfully shout:
  "Jesus saves me now."

Copyright, 1895, by Weeden and Weaver.

116. Whatever You Sow You must Reap.

Words and Music by J. W. VAN DE VENTER.

1. O sinner, take heed, When scattering seed: Whatever you sow you must reap; Wherever it blows, Like thistles it grows, Tho' satan may bury it deep.
2. The moments may fly, The seasons pass by, Your deeds still remaining unknown; But sorrow and tears Will come with the years, Revealing the seed you have sown.
3. It's better to sow Good seed as you go, Then life everlasting is yours. I pray do not wait, The prospects are great, Begin while the promise endures.
4. The seed sowing day Will soon pass away, The angel of death draweth near. Oh, will you not yield, And enter the field, Before the long shadows appear?

CHORUS.

Whatever you sow you must reap, ... you must reap, Whatever you sow you must reap, you must reap! O sinner, take heed, When scattering seed—Whatever you sow you must reap.

Copyright, 1894, by J. W. Van De Venter.

Blind Bartimeus.

Mrs. J. F. K.
Mrs. Joseph F. Knapp.

1. Whence Jesus came, I can-not tell, Nor why He came to me;
2. When all was dark, One touched my eyes, And that is all I know,
3. How it was done, I can-not say, Nor e-ven think nor dream;
4. It is the Son of God! His grace Makes trembling weakness strong;

One thing I know, and know it well; Tho' I was blind I see!
For light came down from par-a-dise And set my soul a-glow.
Nor why a touch of moistened clay Should make things what they seem.
Wipes tears a-way from sorrow's face, And teach-es grief a song.

CHORUS.   ad lib.

I once was blind but now I see! And that is
I once was blind but now I see! And that is
I once was blind but now I see! And that is
I once was blind but now I see! And that is

tempo

news e-nough for me, And that is news e-nough for me.
light e-nough for me, And that is light e-nough for me.
truth e-nough for me, And that is truth e-nough for me.
joy e-nough for me, And that is joy e-nough for me.

By permission. Copyright, 1893, by Mrs. Joseph F. Knapp.

118 We'll Never Say Good-bye.

J. G. D.
J. G. DAILEY.

1. Yes, the sor-row, pain and woe, That we find where'er we go,
2. Ties of friendship, strong and true, Bind your dear-est friend to you;
3. Fa-ther, moth-er, children dear, Whom we've lov'd and cherish'd here,
4. Praise the Lord, the time will come When we'll all be gathered home,

Fill with bit-ter tears the weeping eyes, When we reach the parting strand,
And the hours unheed-ed, swift-ly fly, But the time will come to thee
Wait our com-ing in the by and by; What a meet-ing that will be,
There to live and reign with God on high; End-less prais-es we shall sing,

And we clasp the parting hand, And we sad-ly speak the last good-bye.
When those ties will severed be, And you'll sad-ly speak the last good-bye.
When each oth-er's face we see, And we'll nev-er, nev-er say good-bye.
In the presence of the King, And we'll nev-er, nev-er say good-bye.

CHORUS.

1-2. But we'll never say good-bye, o-ver yonder, We will never say good-
3-4. We will, etc.

bye, o-ver yon-der, As we walk the gold-en street, And each

Used by per. of J. G. Dailey, owner of copyright.

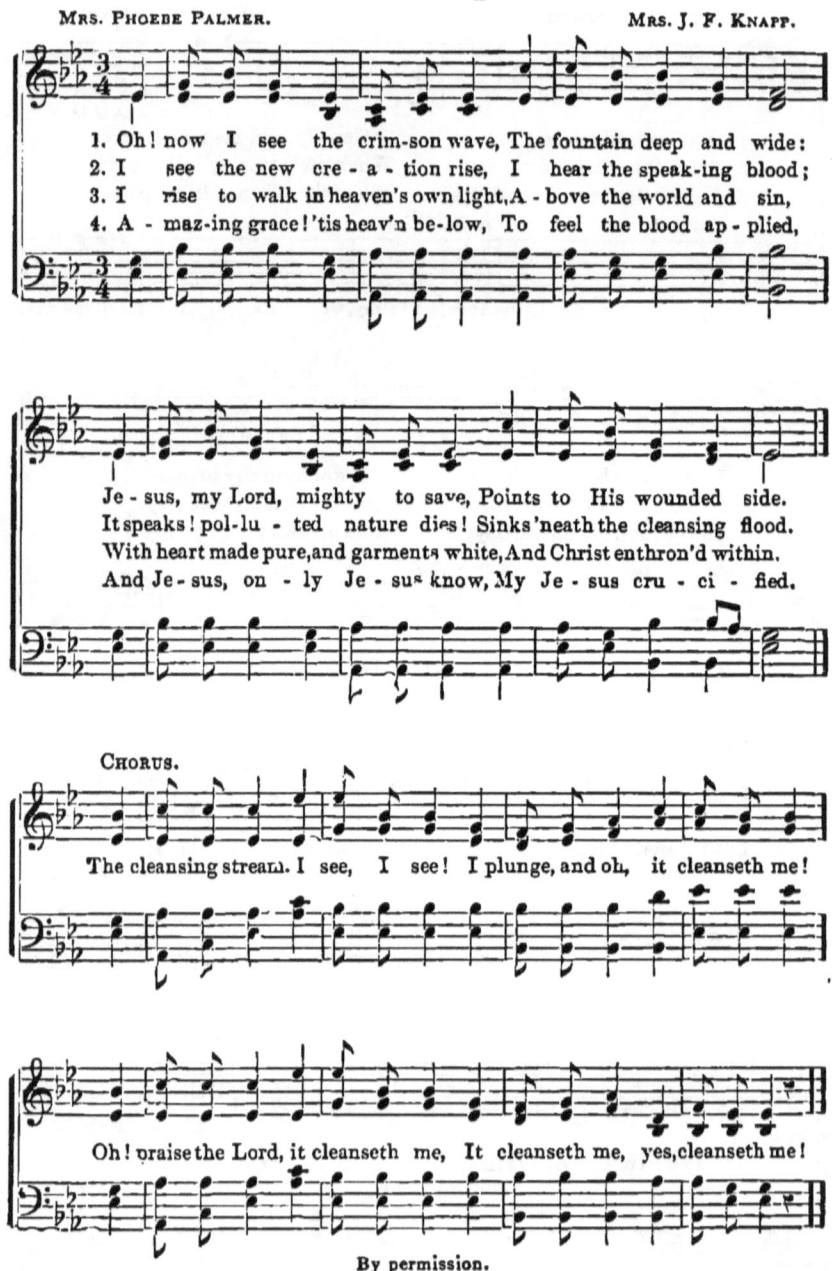

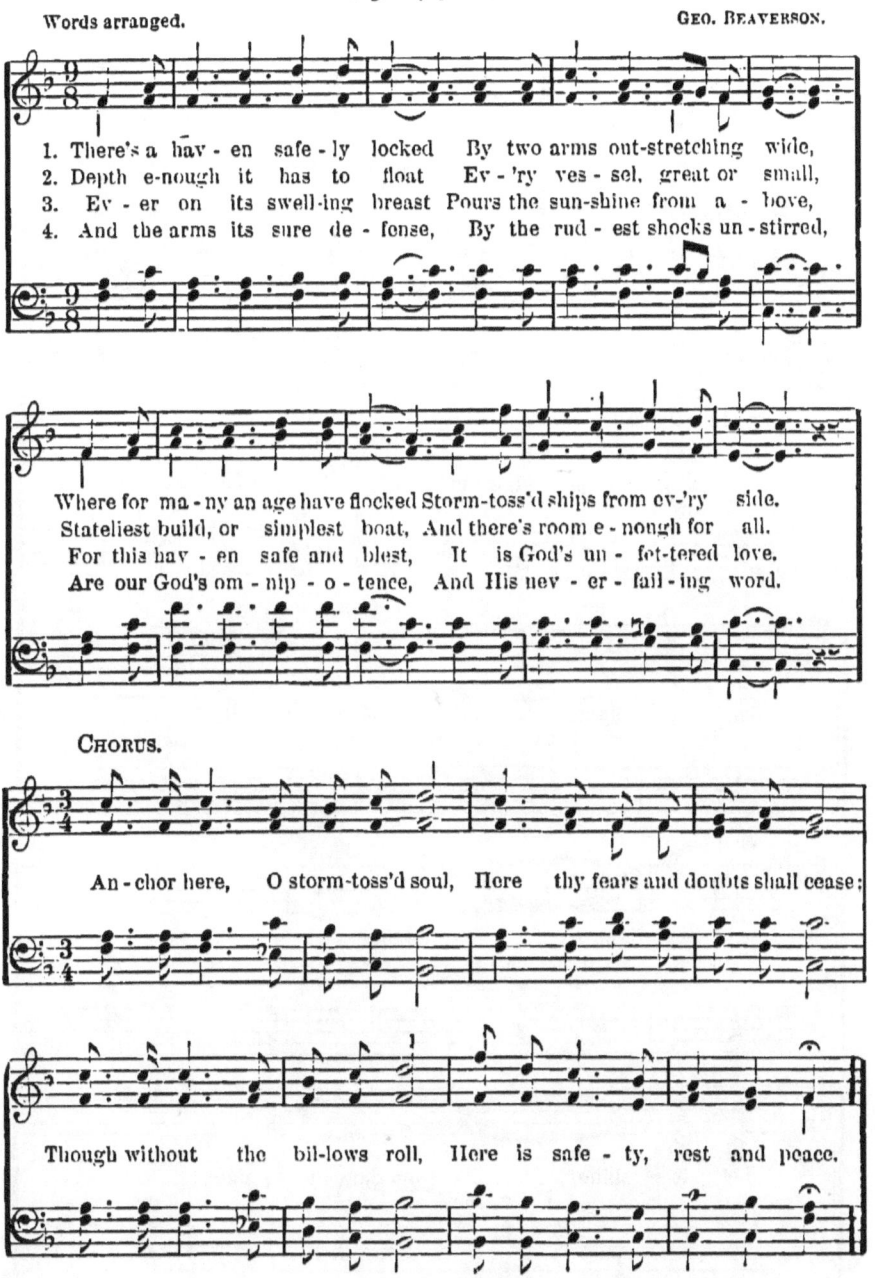

Send the Light. Concluded.

Come to the Savior, Come.

CHAS. WESLEY. ARR. by W. S. WEEDEN.

3 Sent by my Lord, on you I call;
  The invitation is to all.

4 Come all the world! come, sinner, thou
  All things in Christ are ready now.

5 Come, all ye souls by sin oppressed,
  Ye restless wand'rers after rest.

6 Ye poor, and maimed, and halt, and blind
  In Christ a hearty welcome find.

7 My message as from God receive;
  Ye all may come to Christ and live.

8 O let His love your hearts constrain,
  Nor suffer Him to die in vain.

Copyright, 1894, by W. S. Weeden.

For These My Soul Is Lost. Concluded.

CHORUS.

For these poor van-i-ties of life, That soul of price-less cost, Was

Duane Street. L. M., D.

JOHN CENNICK.   Rev. GEORGE COLES.

1. Je-sus, my all, to heav'n is gone, He whom I fix my hopes up-on;
His track I see, and I'll pur-sue The nar-row way, till Him I view.
D.S.—The King's highway of ho-li-ness, I'll go, for all His paths are peace.
The way the ho-ly prophets went, The road that leads from banishment,

2 This is the way I long have sought,
And mourned because I found it not;
My grief a burden long has been,
Because I was not saved from sin.
The more I strove against its power,
I felt its weight and guilt the more;
Till late I heard my Savior say,
"Come hither, soul, I am the way."

3 Lo! glad I come; and thou, blest Lamb,
Shalt take me to Thee, as I am;
Nothing but sin have I to give;
Nothing but love shall I receive.
Then will I tell to sinners 'round,
What a dear Savior I have found;
I'll point to Thy redeeming blood,
And say, "Behold the way to God."

DOXOLOGY—Praise God, from whom all blessings flow;
Praise Him, all creatures here below;
Praise Him, above, ye heavenly host;
Praise Father, Son and Holy Ghost.—THOS. KEN.

Down in the Licensed Saloon.

Answer to "Where is my Wandering Boy To-night?"

Words and Music by W. A. WILLIAMS.

Where is my wand-'ring boy to-night! Down in the licensed sa-loon.

1. Down in a room all co-zy and bright, Filled with the glare of many a light,
2. Little arms once were thrown round my neck, Look at him now, my poor heart will break!
3. Broth-er, I guess you'd en-ter this fight, If it were your boy down there to-night,

Beau-ti-ful mu-sic the ear to de-light, Down in the li-censed sa-loon.
Think of that boy to-night a sad wreck, Down in the li-censed sa-loon.
Ruined and wrecked by the drink appetite, Down in the li-censed sa-loon.

CHORUS.

There is my wand-'ring boy to-night, There is my wand-'ring boy to-night, Down, down, down, down, Down in the licensed sa-loon!

From "Song Jewels," by per.

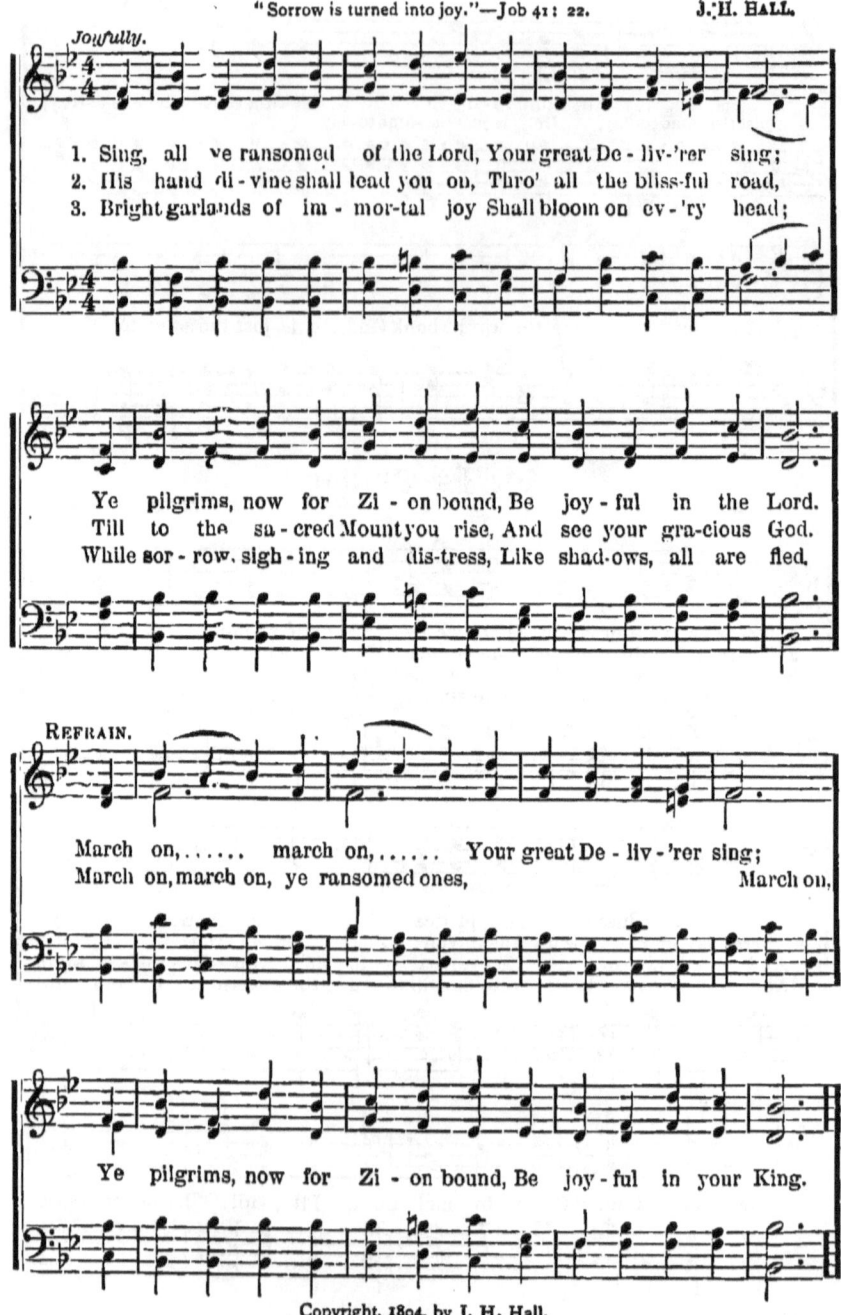

I Need Thee, Lord.

"Without me ye can do nothing."—John xv. 5.

Rev. F. A. Hoffman.   Chas. Edw. Prior.   By per.

1. When cherish'd joys have taken wing, And sorrow wounds me with its sting,
2. When sin has robb'd me of my peace, And bro't me in-to sore dis-tress,
3. When at the cross in anguish bent, An humble, weeping pen-i-tent,
4. When strong temptations come to me To tear my trembling soul from Thee.

    Then to Thy cross   I fond-ly cling, For then   I need Thee, Lord.
    And left me 'reft   of hap-pi-ness, Oh, then   I need Thee, Lord.
    My tears and all   my ef-forts spent, Oh, then   I need Thee, Lord.
    Then to Thy cross for help I flee, For then   I need Thee, Lord.

Chorus.

I need Thee, pre-cious Lord! In Thee my soul would hide!
In ev-'ry time of need, Dear Christ, with me a-bide.

5   When longs my soul for deeper rest,
    To be with all Thy fullness blest,
    I lean me, then, upon Thy breast,
    For then I need Thee, Lord.

6   I need Thee, precious Lord, just now,
    As at the mercy-seat I bow,
    And offer up my solemn vow,
    Just now I need Thee, Lord.

You May, If You Will. Concluded. 149

glo - ry o - ver there, If you will,........ if you will .....
If you will, if you will, if you will.

Come, Sinner, Come.

WILL. E. WITTER.   H. R. PALMER.   By per.

1. While Je - sus whispers to you, Come, sin-ner, come! While we are
2. Are you too hea-vy la-den? Come, sin-ner, come! Je - sus will
3. Oh, hear his ten-der pleading, Come, sin-ner, come! Come and re-

pray-ing for you, Come, sin-ner, come! Now is the time to own Him,
bear your burden. Come, sin-ner, come! Je - sus will not deceive you,
ceive the blessing, Come, sin-ner, come! While Je - sus whispers to you,

Come, sin-ner, come! Now is the time to know Him. Come, sin-ner, come!
Come, sin-ner, come! Je - sus can now redeem you. Come, sin-ner come!
Come, sin-ner, come! While we are pray-ing for you. Come, sin-ner, come!

Copyright, 1879, by H. R. Palmer.

All the Way to Calvary. 151

Mrs. W. G. Moyer & I. H. M.
I. H. Meredith. Cho. arr.

1. Oh, how dark the night that wrapt my spir-it round! Oh, how deep the woe my Sav-ior found When He walked a-cross the wa-ters of my soul, Bade my night dis-perse and made me whole.
2. Tremblingly a sin-ner bowed be-fore his face, Naught I knew of par-don,— God's free grace, Heard a voice so melt-ing, "Cease thy wild re-gret, Je-sus bought thy par-don, paid thy debt."
3. Oh, 'twas wondrous love the Sav-ior show'd for me, When He left His throne for Cal-va-ry, When He trod the wine-press, trod it all a-lone, Praise His name for-ev-er, make it known.

Chorus.

All the way to Cal-va-ry He went for me, He went for me, He went for me, All the way to Cal-va-ry He went for me, He died to set me free.

Copyright, 1894, by I. H. Meredith.

156. Standing by the Cross.

Words by ALLEN SHIRLEY.
REF. by A. J. S.
Music by A. J. SHOWALTER.

1. Sweet the moments, rich in blessing, Which before the cross I spend,
2. Here I'll sit for-ev-er view-ing, Mer-cy streaming in his blood;
3. Tru-ly blessed is this sta-tion, Low before his cross to lie,
4. Here it is I find my heaven, While up-on the cross I gaze,
5. Lord, in ceaseless con-tem-plation, Fix my trusting heart on thee,

Life and health and peace possessing, From the sinner's dying Friend.
Precious drops! my soul bedewing, Plead they now my peace with God.
While I see di-vine compassion, Beaming in his gracious eye.
Here the joy of sins for-giv-en, Shall inspire my songs of praise.
Till I know thy full sal-va-tion, And thy face in glo-ry see.

CHORUS.

Standing by the cross, Standing by the cross, Standing by the cross of Calvary;

Looking up to Christ, Trusting in his love, Hoping in his mercy full and free.

Copyright, 1891, by A. J. Showalter. By per.

Sing On. Concluded.

My heart is fill'd with rap-ture, My soul is lost in praise.

Sing on; O bliss-ful mu - sic, With ev-'ry note you raise,
Sing on; bliss-ful, bliss-ful mu - sic,

My heart is fill'd with rap-ture, My soul is lost in praise.

Aldene. S. M.

Rev. W. L. Wardell. Geo. Beaverson.

1. God always deals in love! Whate'er that dealing be; The soft ca-ress, the stunning blow, Each speak of sym-pa-thy, Each speak of sym-pa-thy.
2. I should not censure God Be-cause I can-not see The reason for the chast'ning rod Which He deems good for me, Which He deems good for me.
3. When in the darksome place He leads my tar-dy feet, No hate is writ-ten on His face; His voice is calm and sweet, His voice is calm and sweet.
4. Tho' death's cold, sullen stream Doth o'er me throw its foam, Yet this or-deal is God's own means To take my spir-it home, To take my spir-it home.

Copyright, 1894, by Geo. Beaverson.

160. When We Reach Our Home.

E. A. H.
Rev. Elisha A. Hoffman.

1. What a scene of wondrous glo-ry, When we reach our home, Chanting there redemption's sto-ry, 'Neath its gold-en dome! With myr-iads round the throne, His a-noint-ed and his own, We will make his prais-es known,
2. We shall know no more of tri - al, When we reach our home, Nor of toil and self-de-ni - al, 'Neath its gold-en dome; In robes of pu - ri-ty, From all sin and sor - row free, Safe with Je - sus we will be
3. We will meet our pre-cious Sav-ior When we reach our home, Live for-ev - er in his fa - vor 'Neath the gold-en dome; Changed to his likeness, we Shall his glo-rious per - son see, And a-dore him cease-less-ly

CHORUS.

When we reach our home.
In our heav'n-ly home. } When we reach our home o-ver there, o-ver there,
In our heav'n-ly home.

All the wondrous glo-ry to share, What a meet-ing that will be o - ver there,

BY PER. OF THE HOFFMAN MUSIC CO.

When We Reach Our Home. Concluded.

When the Savior we shall see, When we reach our home over there, over there.

Nearer to Me.

ELISHA A. HOFFMAN.   WILLIAM A. GALPIN.

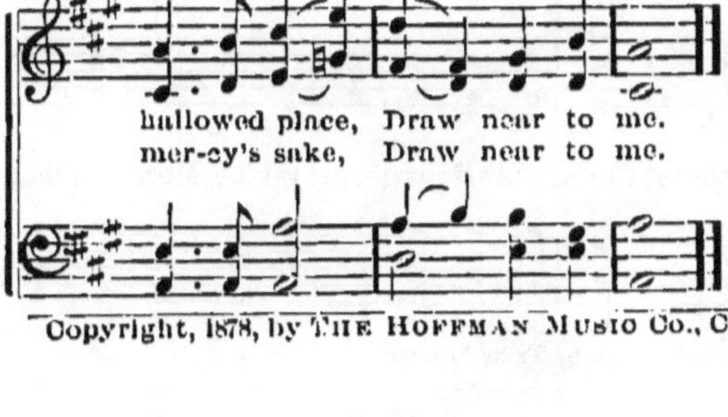

1. Draw near, O Christ, to me, Near-er to me, Un-worth-y and un-clean Though I may be; Come with Thy quick'ning grace, Show me Thy smil-ing face, Draw near this hallowed place, Draw near to me.

2. Draw near, O Christ, to me, Near-er to me, My soul with strong de-sire Burns af-ter Thee; Let me Thy joys par-take, Come, ere my spir-it break, For Thy sweet mer-cy's sake, Draw near to me.

3
Draw near, O Christ, to me,
Nearer to me,
Let all Thy wealth of love
Fall upon me;
Touch every secret sin,
Wash me, and make me clean,
Let nothing stand between
My heart and Thee.

Copyright, 1878, by THE HOFFMAN MUSIC CO., Cleveland.

2 Ask but His grace, and lo ! 'tis giv'n,
I'm at the fountain drinking;
Ask, and He turns your hell to heav'n,
I'm on my journey home.

3 Tho' sin and sorrow wound my soul,
I'm at the fountain drinking,
Jesus, Thy balm will make me whole,
I'm on my journey home.

4 Where'er I am, where'er I move,
I'm at the fountain drinking,
I meet the object of my love,
I'm on my journey home.

5 Insatiate to the spring I fly,
I'm at the fountain drinking;
I drink, and yet am ever dry,
I'm on my journey home.

A Little While with Jesus. Concluded.

I Can, I Will, I Do Believe.

2 Refining fire, go through my heart,
Refining fire, go through my heart,
Refining fire, go through my heart,
Illuminate my soul.

3 O, that it now from heaven might fall,
O, that it now from heaven might fall,
O, that it now from heaven might fall,
And all my sins consume.

166. Leaning on the Everlasting Arms.

REV. E. A. HOFFMAN. A. J. SHOWALTER.

1. What a fel-low-ship, what a joy divine, Lean-ing on the ev-er-lasting arms; What a bless-ed-ness, what a peace is mine,
2. Oh, how sweet to walk in this pilgrim way, Lean-ing on the ev-er-lasting arms; Oh, how bright the path grows from day to day,
3. What have I to dread, what have I to fear, Lean-ing on the ev-er-lasting arms? I have bless-ed peace with my Lord so near,

Lean-ing on the ev-er-last-ing arms.

REFRAIN.

Lean - - ing, lean - - ing, Safe and se-cure from all a-larms; Lean - - ing, lean - - ing, Lean-ing on the ev-er-last-ing arms. Leaning on Jesus, leaning on Jesus, Leaning on Jesus, Leaning on Jesus,

Copyright, by A. J. Showalter. By per.

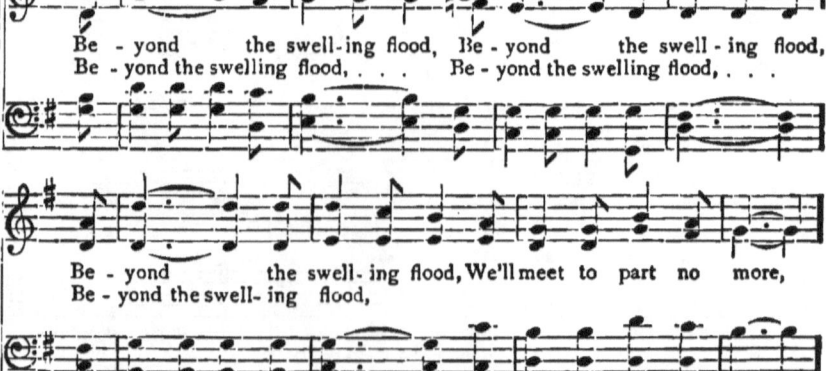

Beyond the Swelling Flood. Concluded.

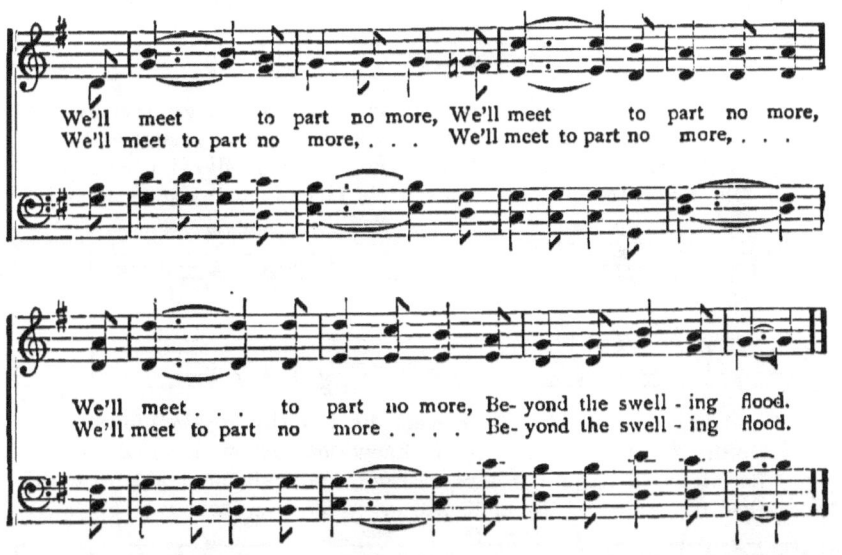

Good Night.
AVON. C. M.

JOHN McPHERSON.   Scottish.

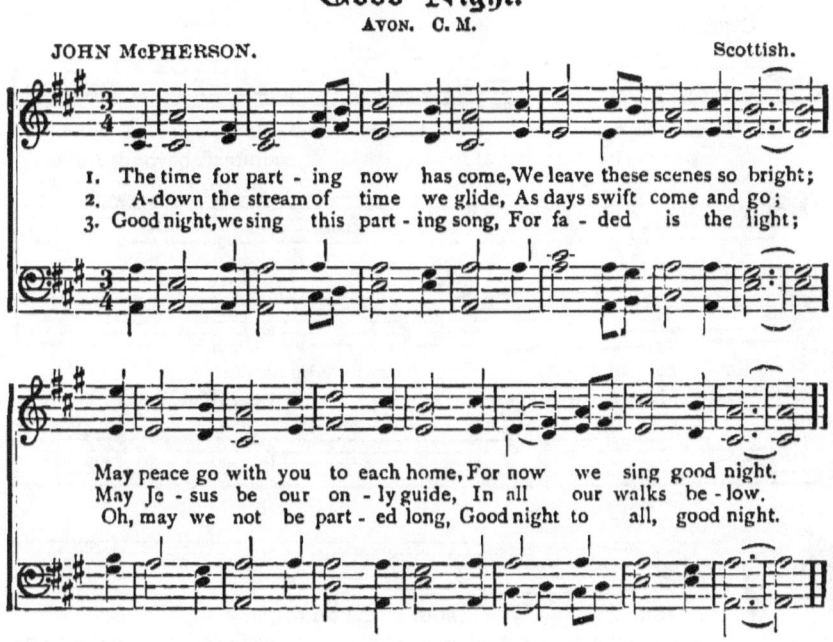

Wonderful Love. Concluded.

To save . . . . a poor sinner like me.
save a poor sinner like me, like me, a sin-ner like me.

Cling.

Anon.   GEO. BEAVERSON.

1. Cling to the Might-y One, Cling in thy grief, Cling to the Ho-ly One, He gives re-lief: Cling to the Gracious One, Cling in thy pain; Cling to the Faithful One, He will sus-tain.
2. Cling to the Liv-ing One, Cling in thy woe; Cling to the Liv-ing One, Through all be-low; Cling to the Pardoning One, He speaketh peace, Cling to the Healing One, Anguish shall cease.
3. Cling to the Bleed-ing One, Cling to His side, Cling to the Ris-en One, In Him a-bide; Cling to the Com-ing One, Hope shall a-rise, Cling to the Reigning One, Joy lights thine eyes.

Copyright, 1894, by Geo. Beaverson.

172. Steadily Marching On.

FANNY J. CROSBY.   H. R. PALMER. By per.

1. Praise ye the Lord! joy-ful-ly shout ho-san-na! Praise the Lord with glad acclaim;
2. Praise we the Lord! He is the King e-ter-nal; Glo-ry be to God on high!

Lift up our hearts un-to His throne with gladness,—Magni-fy His ho-ly name.
Praise we the Lord, tell of His lov-ing kindness,—Join the chorus of the sky.

Marching a-long under His banner bright, Trusting in His mercy as we go, *trusting we go,*
Still marching on, cheerily marching on, In the ranks of Je-sus we will go, *ever we'll go,*

His light di-vine ten-der-ly o'er us will shine; We shall be guid-ed by His
Home to our rest, joy-ful-ly home, where the blest Gath-er and praise the Savior's

hand now and for-ev - er. }
name, praise Him for-ev - er. } Stead-i-ly marching on, with our ban-ner waving o'er us,

CHORUS.

Stead-i-ly marching on, while we sing the joy-ful cho-rus; Stead-i-ly marching

on, pil-lar and cloud going be-fore us, To the realms of glo-ry, to our home on high.

Copyright, 1881, by H. R. Palmer.

I Have It in My Soul, Hallelujah!

Dedicated to my friend, William P. Pratt, Portland, Maine.

E. S. U.
Rev. E. S. UFFORD.

1. Come, weep just as we did in sor-row for sin, Come, knock till the Lord bid you en-ter within; Come trust-ing, ex-pect-ing, There's no oth-er way, And soon you will find it the gladsome new day.
2. Come, pray just as we did to live hour by hour, Above earth's temptations, with God's keeping pow'r; To kneel oft in prayer is vic-t'ry be-gun, Thus wrestling with e-vil the crown will be won.
3. Come, shout just as we did your "Glo-ry to God!" Sing prais-es to Je-sus, who saves by His blood; The song of re-demption shall be our re-frain, Till in the new heaven we sing it a-gain.

CHORUS.

I have it in my soul, hal-le-lu-jah! I have found the Savior precious all the way, all the way, I was once a child of sin, but I let my Savior in, And there's sunlight in my soul to-day.

Copyright, 1894, by E. S. Ufford.

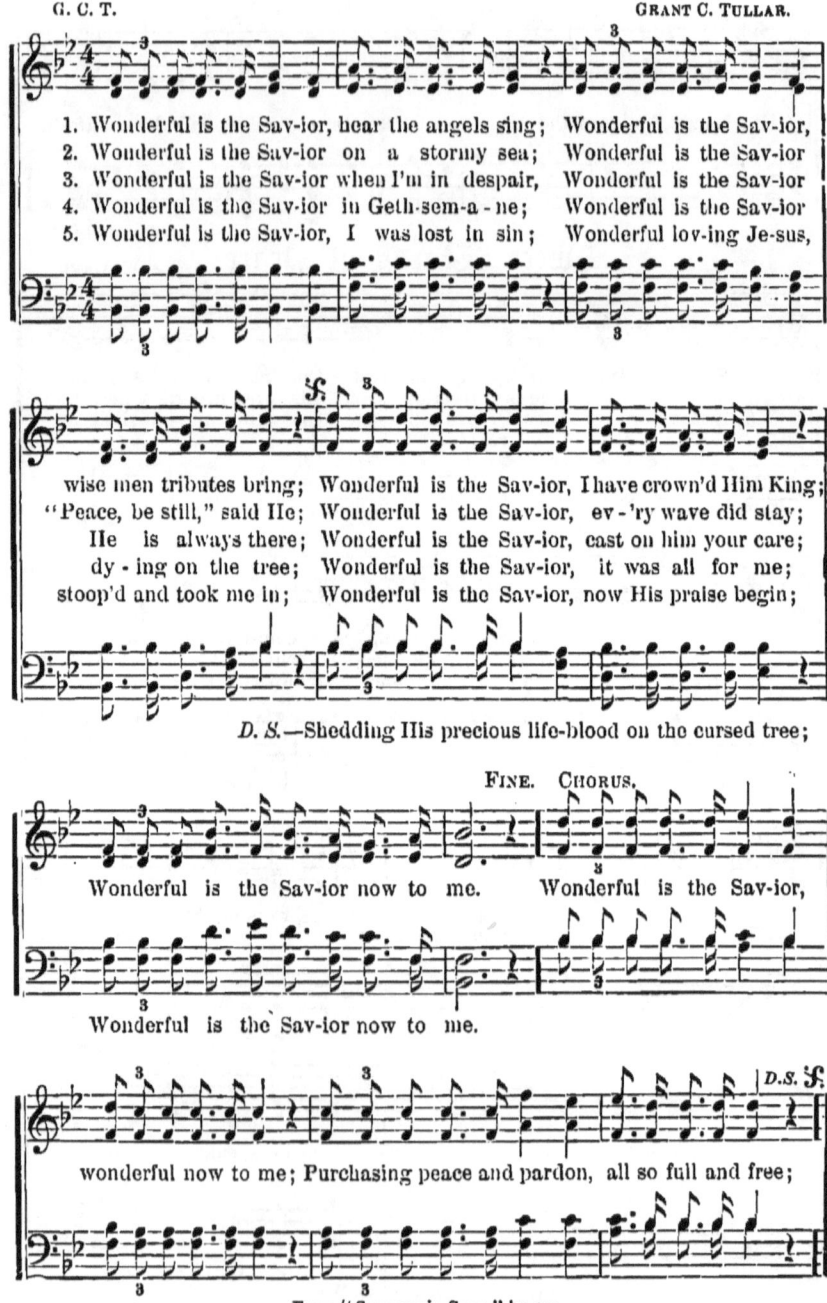

186. Sabbath Day Song.

B. W. CAMP.   J. H. ALLEMAN.

1. O beau-ti-ful day, bright Sab-bath day That Jesus hath giv'n for rest, His word let us search for truths that we may By faith in His promise be blest.
2. Our la-bors and cares we'll lay a-side, Our hearts un-to Him we'll bring; We'll turn from the world, its fol-lies de-ride, To hon-or the Sav-ior, our King.
3. We'll sing of the day, dear Sab-bath day That Jesus, the Lord hath blest; From earth and its cares we're pass-ing a-way To en-ter the Sab-bath of rest.

CHORUS.

We'll sing of the beau-ti-ful Sab-bath day, The day of all oth-ers the best, 'Till Jesus shall call His dear children a-way To en-ter the Sab-bath of rest.

Used by per. of J. H. Alleman, Publisher, Chicago, Ill.

188. Sowing the Tares.

Dedicated to "Brother Will," M. Cell 1069.

Words by a Convict.
M. A. Lee.

Slow. To be sung as a Solo.

1. Sow-ing the tares, when it might have been wheat, Sowing of mal-ice, spite, and de-ceit, We might have sown ro-ses a-mid life's sad cares, While we were so cru-el-ly sow-ing the tares;
2. Sow-ing the tares, how dark the black sin, Mingling a curse with life's sweetest hymn, And heeding no an-guish, no pit-e-ous pray'rs, While we were so cru-el-ly sow-ing the tares;
3. Sow-ing the tares that bring sor-row down, Robs of its jew-els life's fair-est crown; And turning to sil-ver the once golden hairs, Grown whit-er and whit-er as we sowed the tares;
4. Sow-ing the tares un-der cov-er of night, Which might have been wheat, all golden and bright; O heart, turn to God with repentance and pray'r, And plead for for-give-ness for sow-ing the tares;

REFRAIN.

Sow-ing the tares, Sow-ing the tares, We plead for for-give-ness for sow-ing the tares.

From "Rescue Songs." Used by per. of H. H. Hadley.

The Sinner and the Song.

By Will L. Thompson.

Quartet, to be sung very softly.

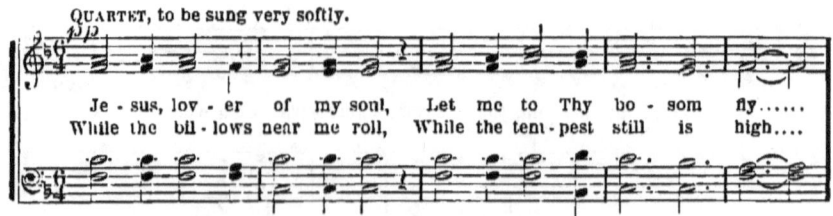

From "Thompson's Popular Anthems," Copyrighted and Published by
Will L. Thompson, East Liverpool, Ohio.

The Sinner and the Song. Concluded.

The Day of Jubilee. Concluded.

When the Roll Is Called, etc. Concluded

The Fountain Now is Open.

Rev. Jos. Hart, 1759.   Arr. by J. W. Van De Venter.

1. { Come, ye sin-ners, poor and needy, Weak and wounded, sick and sore; }
   { Je-sus read-y stands to save you, Full of pi-ty, love, and power; }
2. { Now, ye need-y, come and welcome; God's free bounty glo-ri-fy; }
   { True be-lief and true repent-ance,—Ev'ry grace that brings you nigh; }

CHORUS.

For the foun-tain now is o-pen, the foun-tain now is o-pen,
The foun-tain now is o-pen, O sin-ner, won't you come?

3 Let not conscience make you linger;
  Nor of fitness fondly dream;
  All the fitness He requireth
  Is to feel your need of Him;

4 Come, ye weary, heavy-laden,
  Bruised and mangled by the fall;
  If you tarry till you're better,
  You will never come at all;

Copyright, 1894, by J. W. Van De Venter.

Raise the Song Triumphant.

Play first four measures for prelude. Words and music by GEO. NOYES ROCKWELL.

VOICES IN UNISON. *Spirited.*

1. Raise the song tri-umph-ant, Sing in cho-rus strong; Let all earth re-ech-o
2. Tho' sin and temp-ta-tion Ev-'rywhere abound, Tho' the hosts of Sa-tan
3. Would we reign in glo-ry, And a crown there wear, We must here be faith-ful

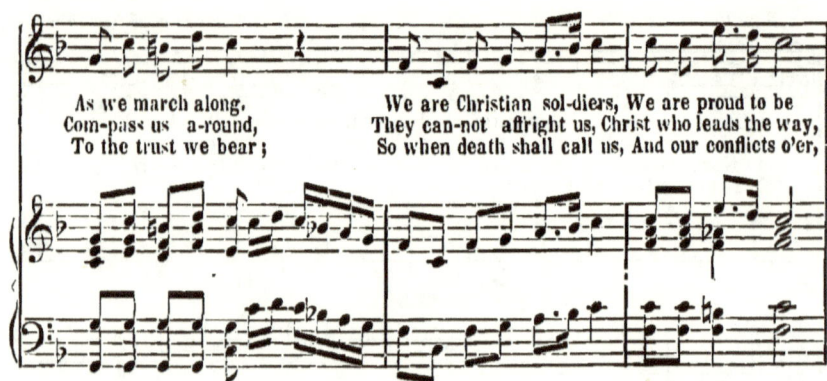

As we march along, We are Christian sol-diers, We are proud to be
Com-pass us a-round, They can-not affright us, Christ who leads the way,
To the trust we bear; So when death shall call us, And our conflicts o'er,

CHORUS.

Foll'wers of a Cap-tain Who has made us free,
Conquer'd them, and by Him We shall gain the day. Then march on to bat-tle,
We shall reign in glo-ry, Vic-tors ev-er-more.

From "Songs of Y. W. C. Temperance Union," by per.

202. Jesus Is Passing This Way.

E. A. H.
J. H. T.

1. Is there a sin-ner a-wait-ing Mer-cy and pardon to-day?
2. Brother, the Master is wait-ing, Waiting to free-ly for-give;
3. Yes, he is coming to bless you While in contrition you bow;

Welcome the news that we bring him: "Jesus is passing this way!"
Why not this moment accept him, Trust in his grace and live?
Coming from sin to re-deem you, Read-y to save you now;

Coming in love and in mer-cy, Pardon and peace to be-stow,
He is so tender and pre-cious, He is so near you to-day;
Can you re-fuse the sal-va-tion Je-sus is of-fer-ing here?

Coming to save the poor sin-ner From his heart-anguish and woe.
O-pen your heart to receive him, While he is passing this way.
O-pen your heart to ad-mit him, While he is coming so near.

Chorus.

Je-sus is passing this way...... To-day,........ to-day,
Jesus is passing this way, To-day, is passing to-day!

Jesus is Passing This Way. Concluded.

While he is near, O be-lieve him, O-pen your heart to receive him, For

Je-sus is passing this way, this way, Is passing this way to-day.

The Way, the Truth, the Life.

E. R. LATTA.   J. H. T.

1. "I am the way," the Savior said; The paths of sin forsake;
  Slumber no more in error's night, In . . . . . righteousness awake.
2. "I am the truth," the Savior said; In faith draw near to me;
  He that believeth shall be saved, The . . . . truth shall make him free.
3. "I am the life," the Savior said, Your sins and sorrows leave;
  Shun ye the path that leads to death; E - - - - ter-nal life receive.

Chorus.

Sinner to-day   Hear Jesus say: I am the way, the truth, the life,

Sinner to-day   Hear Jesus say: I am the way, the truth, the life.

I Am Trusting in My Savior. 205

LEONARD WEAVER, Evangelist.   J. W. WARD.

1. I am trust-ing in my Sav-ior, For his death up-on the tree;
2. I am look-ing un-to Je-sus, To sup-ply all dai-ly grace;

Has re-moved all condem-na-tion, And from sin has set me free.
And so sweet-ly I am rest-ing In the sun-shine of His face.

CHORUS.
Rest-ing so sweet-ly, Foll'-wing so close-ly,
Kept for His ser-vice I e'er would be, Wait-ing and watching,
Work-ing and prais-ing 'Till in the glo-ry His face I see.

3 I am living now to serve Him,
   Go or wait at His command;
   Like a servant, ever ready
   To obey I listening stand.

4 I am working for the Master
   In the harvest field to-day;
   Oh, how sweet it is to follow,
   When His Spirit leads the way.

5 I am following in the foot-prints
   He has left along the way;
   And, tho' rough at times the journey
   Yet it leads to endless day.

6 I am waiting for His coming,
   When the working day is o'er;
   I am watching and I'm longing,
   To be with Him evermore.

Copyright, 1894, by W. S. Weeden.

Are You Walking in the Light? Concluded.

Hark! Ten Thousand Harps.

T. KELLY.   HARWELL. 8s. & 7s. 8 lines.   LOWELL MASON.

3 King of glory, reign forever;
   Thine an everlasting crown;
 Nothing from Thy love shall sever,
   Those whom Thou hast made Thine
 Happy object of thy grace,   [own,
 Chosen to behold His face.

4 Saviour hasten thine appearing,
   Bring O bring the glorious day;
 When the awful summons hearing,
   Heaven and earth shall pass away;
 Then with golden harps will sing,
 " Glory, glory to our King."

208. Building Day by Day.

HENRIETTA E. BLAIR.   HERBERT D. LOTHROP.

1. We are build-ing in sor-row, and build-ing in joy, A tem-ple the world cannot see; But we know it will stand if we found it on a rock, Thro' the a-ges of e-ter-ni-ty.
2. Ev-'ry deed forms a part in this build-ing of ours, That is done in the name of the Lord; For the love that we show and the kindness we be-stow, He has promised us a bright re-ward.
3. Then be watch-ful and wise, let the tem-ple we rear Be one that no tem-pest can shock; For the Mas-ter has said and He taught us in His word, We must build upon the sol-id rock.

CHORUS.

We are building day by day, As the moments glide away, Our temple which the world may not see; Ev-'ry vic-t'ry won by grace Will be

Copyright, 1891, by Wm. J. Kirkpatrick.

Farewell.

J. W. VAN DE VENTER.

J. KINKLE. Arr. by G. B.

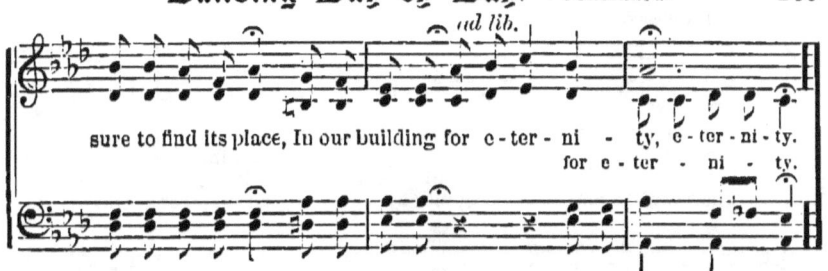

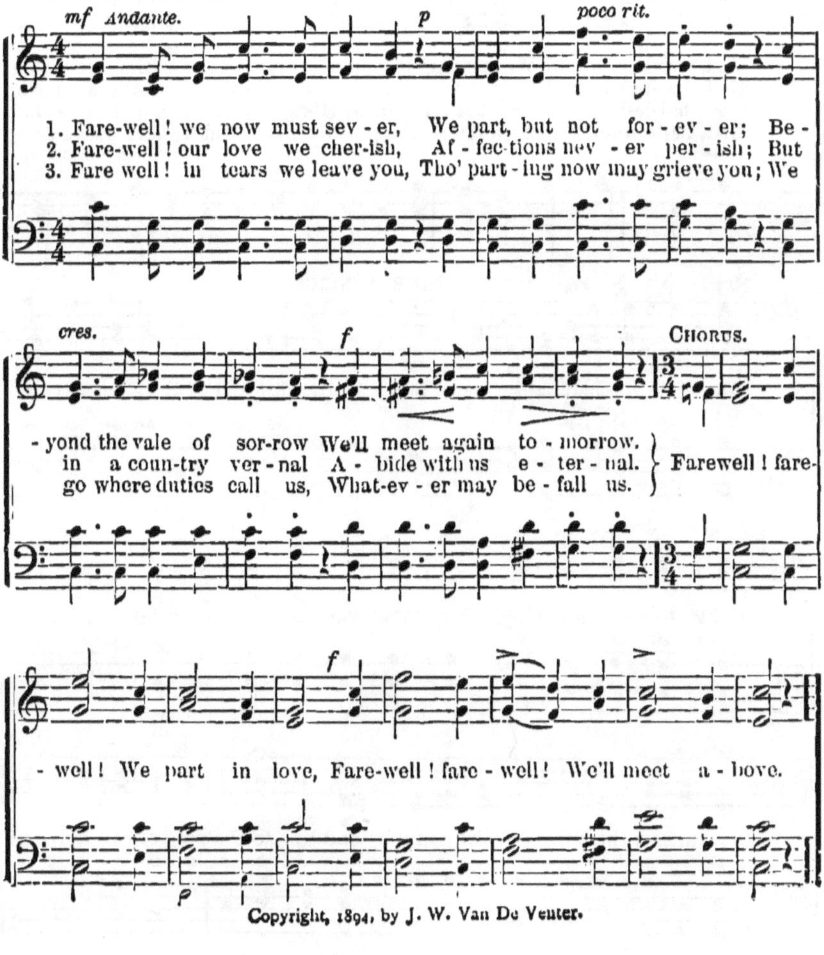

My Heart's Prayer. 211

"Lord, I believe, help Thou mine unbelief."—Mark 9: 24.

FLORA McLEAN. Arr. by W. G. C.   Rev. W. G. COOPER.

1. Dear Lord, in-crease my faith, I pray, While on this earth I roam;
Ban-ish my ev-'ry doubt a-way, And guide me safe-ly home.
Guide me home, guide me home, Guide me safe-ly home;
Ban-ish my ev-'ry doubt a-way, And guide me safe-ly home.

2. Give me the faith to trust Thy pow'r, E'en where I can-not see;
The faith to yield, this ve-ry hour, My life, my all to Thee.
All to Thee, all to Thee, Life and all to Thee;
Help me to yield this ve-ry hour, My life and all to Thee.

3. To yield the whole and not a part, Is my most earn-est pray'r;
Come, Thou, and cleanse my froward heart, And reign for-ev-er there.
Cleanse my heart, cleanse my heart, Reign for-ev-er there;
Come, Thou, and cleanse my fro-ward heart, And reign for-ev-er there.

4. Should an-y-thing e'er seem to stand Be-tween Thy heart and mine,
Spare not the chast'ning of Thy hand, Till I am whol-ly Thine.
Whol-ly Thine, whol-ly Thine, Till I'm whol-ly Thine;
Spare not the chast'ning of Thy hand, Till I am whol-ly Thine.

5 Then, when on earth my work is past,
   And I have reached the goal,
Oh, bear me to my home at last,
   An humble, grateful soul.
Bear me home, bear me home,
   To my heav'nly home;
Oh, bear me to my home at last,
   An humble, grateful soul.

6 A palm of victory I'll bear,
   Of victory over sin;
And I shall tell the angels there,
   How Jesus took me in.
Tell them there, tell them there,
   Jesus took me in;
Oh, I shall tell the angels there,
   How Jesus took me in.

From "Pearls of Paradise," by per.

They are Covered by the Blood. 213

L. E. JONES.   I. H. MEREDITH.

1. I brought my sins to Cal - va - ry, They are cov-ered by the blood of Je - sus; There He in mer - cy set me free, They are
2. My woes are bur - ied 'neath the tide, They are cov-ered by the blood of Je - sus; Be - neath the foun - tain deep and wide, They are
3. 'Twas my trans-gres-sions that He bore, They are cov-ered by the blood of Je - sus; Now He re - mem-bers them no more, They are
4. The bur - dens that my soul op-prest, They are cov-ered by the blood of Je - sus; He took them all and gave me rest, They are

CHORUS.

cov-ered by the blood of Je - sus, They are cov-ered by the blood, cov-ered by the blood, Cov-ered by the blood of Je - sus; Tho' crim-son were my sins I know, They are covered by the blood of Je - sus.

Copyright, 1894, by I. H. Meredith.

The Lost Soul's Lament — Concluded

The har - - vest is end - - ed, And I am not saved.
har-vest is end - ed, the har-vest is end- ed,

5 I stretch out my weak helpless hand | Where loving friends wait for me; [brav'd
Far, far toward the jasper sea, | Whose kind faithful warnings, I often have
And pray one glimpse of that radiant land-- | But the harvest is ended and I am not sav'd.

Welcome Evening Shadows.

IDA L. REED.   H. N. LINCOLN.

1. Welcome evening shad-ows, Welcome twi-light gray, Sun-set tints are
2. Welcome evening shad-ows, Fall-ing si-lent-ly, Like a veil a-
3. Welcome shades of eve-ning, Fall-ing one by one, Day is soft-ly

fad- ing, Dy-ing is the day; And the way-worn toil-ers,
bout us, Shel-tered thus we'll be; Fold our man-tles o'er us,
dy- ing, All its toil is done; Wel-come twi-light shad-ows,

Glad-ly one by one, Turn their fa-ces home-ward, Day's long toil is done.
And se-cure-ly rest, By thy mer-cy guard-ed, Saviour we are blest.
Life is al-most o'er, Soon we'll wake in glad-ness, On the farther shore.

Copyright, 1892, by H. N. Lincoln.   From "Song Land Messenger," by per. of H. N. Lincoln.

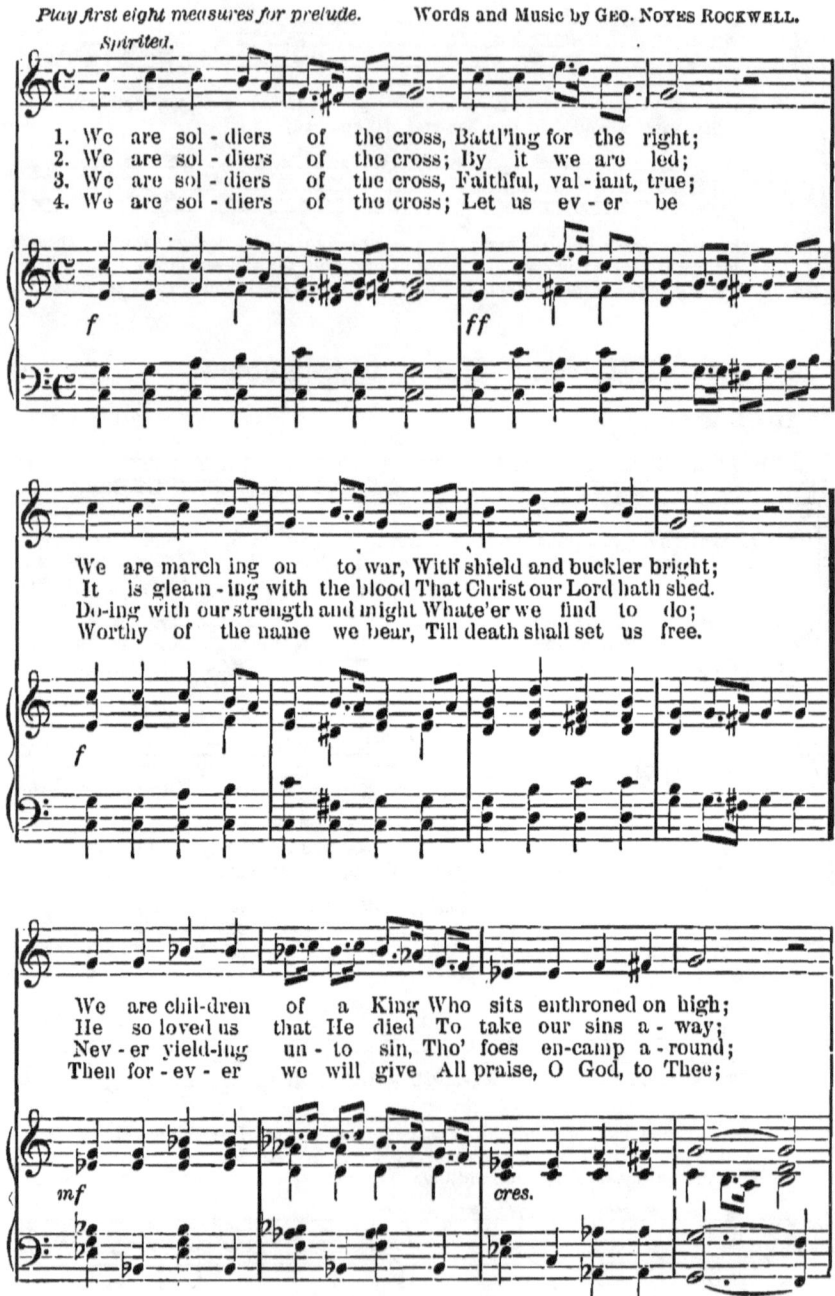

We are Soldiers of the Cross. Concluded. 217

He is strong, and we shall win If on Him we re - ly.
It is lit - tle we can do This debt of love to pay.
Us - ing prayer, a wea-pon strong, To crush them to the ground.
Fa - ther, Son, and Ho - ly Ghost, The bless - ed Trin - i - ty.

CHORUS.
As we march ring out the song, Lift the cross on high;
Blow the trum-pet loud and long, And shout the bat-tle cry.

Angels Hovering Round.

1 There are angels hov'ring round, etc.
2 To carry the tidings home, etc.
3 To the New Jerusalem, etc.
4 Poor sinners are coming home, etc.
5 And Jesus bids them come, etc.
6 There's glory all around, etc.

218. The Bleeding Lamb.

Arranged by G. B.

1. My Sav-ior died up-on the tree,
   Oh, come and praise the Lord with me,
   Glo-ry to the bleeding Lamb.
   D. C.—It sets my spir-it all a-flame, Glo-ry to the bleeding Lamb.

CHORUS.
The Lamb, the Lamb, the bleeding Lamb, I love the sound of Je-sus' name;

2 I know my sins are all forgiven,
   Glory to the bleeding Lamb,
   And I am on my way to heaven,
   Glory to the bleeding Lamb.

3 Now I will tell to sinners 'round,
   Glory to the bleeding Lamb;
   What a dear Savior I have found,
   Glory to the bleeding Lamb.

4 His blood has washed my sins away,
   Glory to the bleeding Lamb,
   And I can sing as well as pray,
   Glory to the bleeding Lamb.

5 I point to Thy redeeming blood,
   Glory to the bleeding Lamb,
   And shout, behold the way to God,
   Glory to the bleeding Lamb.

219. We'll Work till Jesus Comes.

Dr. MILLER.

1. O land of rest, for thee I sigh, When will the moment come,
   When I shall lay my ar-mor by, And dwell in peace.......... at home?
2. No tranquil joys on earth I know, No peaceful, shelt'ring dome,
   This world's a wil-der-ness of woe, This world is not my ...... my home.
3. To Je-sus Christ I fled for rest; He bade me cease to roam,
   And lean for suc-cor on His breast, And He'd conduct .... me home.

CHORUS.
We'll work till Je-sus comes, We'll work till Je-sus comes,

Copyright, 1895, by Weeden and Weaver.

1 'Tis My All.

HARRIET McEWEN KIMBALL. Alt. — Rev. ELISHA A. HOFFMAN.

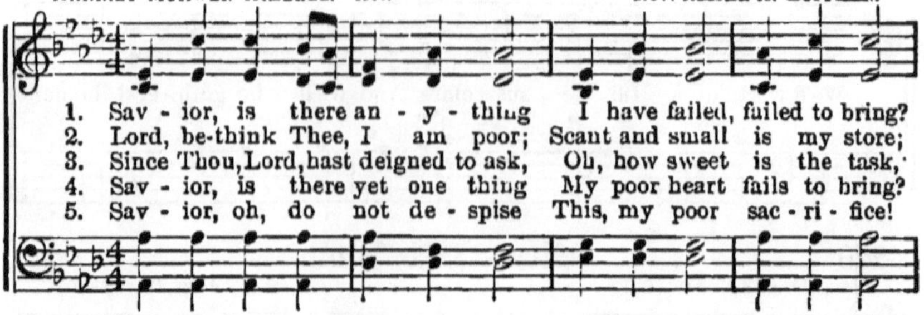

1. Sav-ior, is there an-y-thing I have failed, failed to bring?
2. Lord, be-think Thee, I am poor; Scant and small is my store;
3. Since Thou, Lord, hast deigned to ask, Oh, how sweet is the task,
4. Sav-ior, is there yet one thing My poor heart fails to bring?
5. Sav-ior, oh, do not de-spise This, my poor sac-ri-fice!

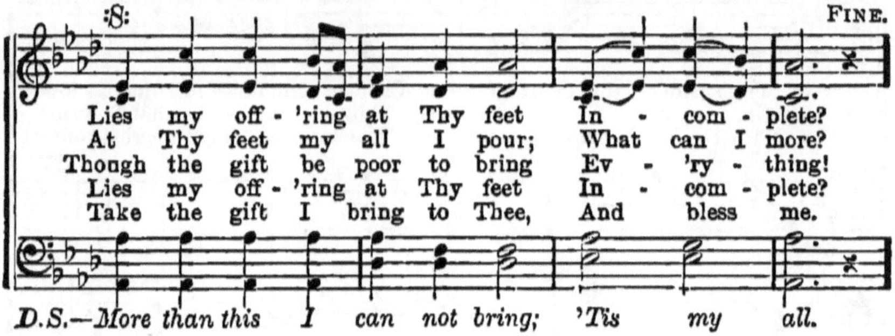

Lies my off-'ring at Thy feet In-com-plete?
At Thy feet my all I pour; What can I more?
Though the gift be poor to bring Ev-'ry-thing!
Lies my off-'ring at Thy feet In-com-plete?
Take the gift I bring to Thee, And bless me.

D.S.—More than this I can not bring; 'Tis my all.

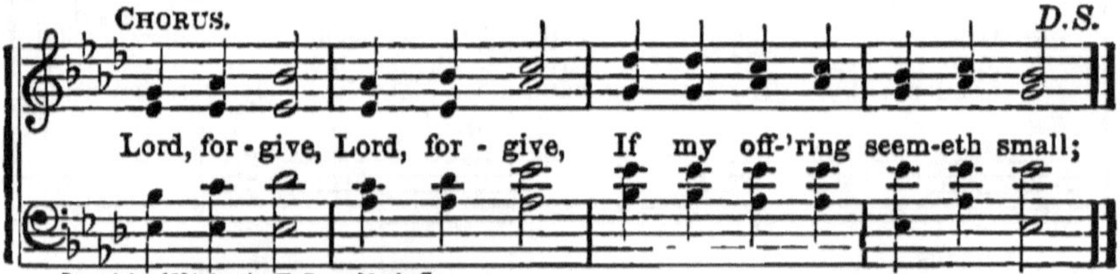

CHORUS.

Lord, for-give, Lord, for-give, If my off-'ring seem-eth small;

Copyright, 1894, by the Hoffman Music Co.

222 What Work Hast Thou for Me?

ELISHA R. PETTIT. — FRANK M. DAVIS.

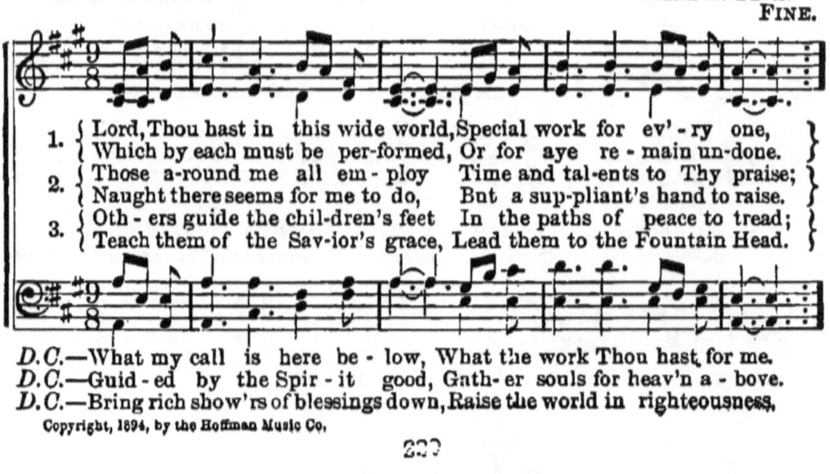

1. { Lord, Thou hast in this wide world, Special work for ev'-ry one,
    { Which by each must be per-formed, Or for aye re-main un-done.
2. { Those a-round me all em-ploy Time and tal-ents to Thy praise;
    { Naught there seems for me to do, But a sup-pliant's hand to raise.
3. { Oth-ers guide the chil-dren's feet In the paths of peace to tread;
    { Teach them of the Sav-ior's grace, Lead them to the Fountain Head.

D.C.—What my call is here be-low, What the work Thou hast for me.
D.C.—Guid-ed by the Spir-it good, Gath-er souls for heav'n a-bove.
D.C.—Bring rich show'rs of blessings down, Raise the world in righteousness.

Copyright, 1894, by the Hoffman Music Co.

What Work Hast Thou for Me? Concluded.

4 Some in self-denial live,
   Ever gentle, good and kind,
  "Raise the fallen, cheer the faint,
   Heal the sick, and lead the blind."
  Each has noble work to do;
  Each fulfils his chosen part;
  Naught there seems for me to do,—
   Naught that can inspire my heart.

5 Give me some great work to do,
   And Thy grace and strength impart;
  Let me labor in Thy cause,
   With Thy love within my heart;
  Or, some little thing, if Thou
   Choosest it as best for me;
  Only let me labor now,
   And thus show my love to Thee.

223 Trusting in His Faithfulness.

E A. H.   Rev. Elisha A. Hoffman.

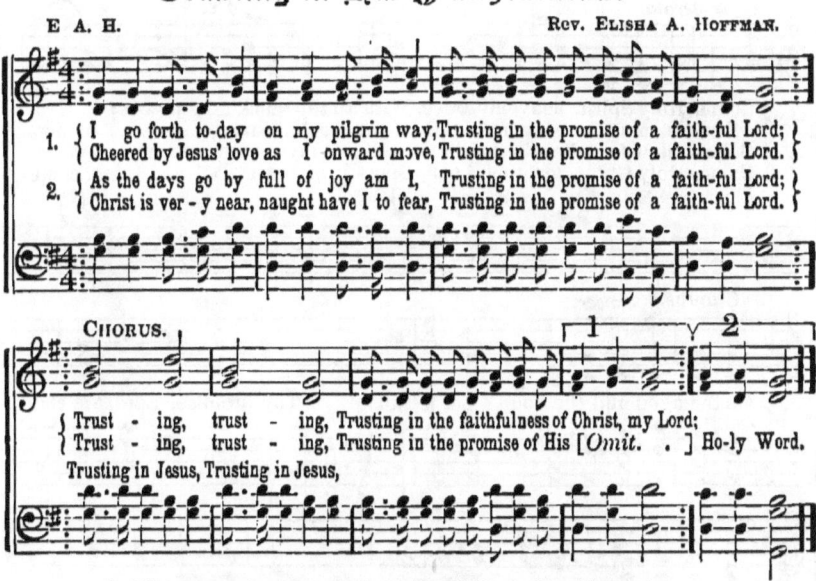

3 All is now at rest, saved am I and blest, Trusting, etc.;
  Helped from heav'n above, strong in faith and love, Trusting, etc.

4 Deeper peace I know as I forward go, Trusting, etc.;
  'Neath His mighty arm, what can do me harm, Trusting, etc.

5 Oh, the happiness! oh, the wondrous bliss, Trusting, etc.!
  Oh, the comfort sweet! oh, the rest complete, Trusting, etc.!

6 So I journey on till life's work is done, Trusting, etc.,
  Till the race is run and the crown is won, Trusting, etc.

Copyright, 1894, by the Hoffman Music Co.

224. I'm Glad Salvation's Free.

Arr. by G. B.

1 I'm glad salvation's free,
    And without price or cost,
   For had it been for me to buy,
    My soul must have been lost.

Cho.—I'm glad salvation's free,
    I'm glad salvation's free,
   Salvation's free for you and me,
    I'm glad salvation's free.

2 In this cold world below,
    With none to care for me,
   A pilgrim lone, without a home—
    I'm glad salvation's free.

3 Once I was blind and lost,
    Of sin and sorrow full;
   But now I'm saved thro' Jesus' blood,
    I feel it in my soul.

4 And now I'm on the way
    To brighter worlds above;
   I hope to triumph evermore
    Through the Redeemer's love.

225. Let It Fall.

I. WATTS, 1 and 4.
C. WESLEY, 2 and 3. } Chorus and Melody furnished by L. W.   Arr. by G. B.

Moderato. Acts i. 8.

1. { Come, Holy Spirit, heavenly Dove, With all thy quick'ning pow'rs;
     Kindle a flame of sacred love In these cold hearts............of ours. }
2. { O that it now from heav'n might fall, And all my sins consume!
     Come, Holy Ghost, for thee I call, Spir-it of burn - - ing, come! }

CHORUS. *Slower.*

On the aged and the young Let it fall! Thy promise, Lord, we claim;
It will guide us on to truth, Let it fall! And sanc-ti-fy us all.

3 Refining fire, go through my heart,
    Illuminate my soul;
   Scatter thy life through every part,
    And sanctify the whole.

4 Come, Holy Spirit, heavenly Dove,
    With all thy quickening powers;
   Come, shed abroad a Savior's love,
    And that shall kindle ours.

Copyright, 1895, by Weeden and Weaver.

226. Heaven is My Home.

Scotch Air.

Adagio e Legato.

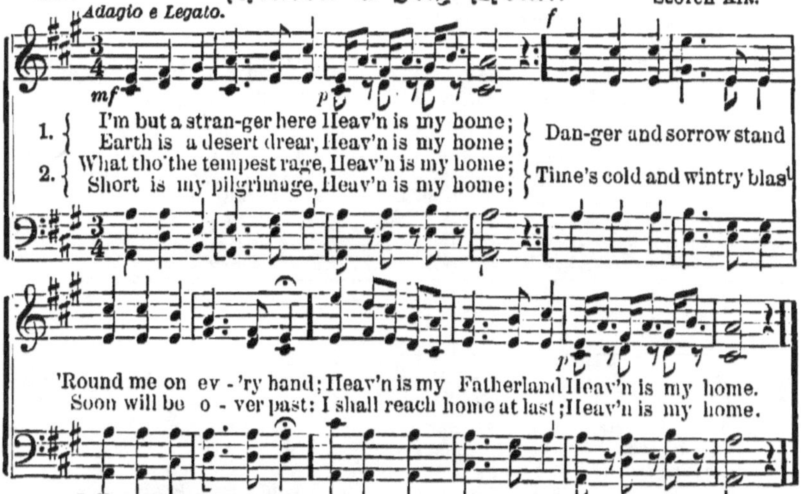

1. I'm but a stran-ger here, Heav'n is my home;
   Earth is a desert drear, Heav'n is my home;
   Dan-ger and sorrow stand
2. What tho' the tempest rage, Heav'n is my home;
   Short is my pilgrimage, Heav'n is my home;
   Time's cold and wintry blast

'Round me on ev-'ry hand; Heav'n is my Fatherland, Heav'n is my home.
Soon will be o-ver past: I shall reach home at last; Heav'n is my home.

3 Peace! O my troubled soul,
   Heav'n is my home;
   I soon shall reach the goal;
   Heav'n is my home;
   Swiftly the race I'll run.
   Yield up my crown to none:
   Forward! the prize is won;
   Heav'n is my home.

4 There, at my Savior's side,
   Heav'n is my home;
   I shall be glorified;
   Heav'n is my home;
   There are the good and blest,
   Those I loved most and best,
   There, too, I soon shall rest,
   Heav'n is my home.

NOTE:—The words "Nearer My God to Thee," are admirably adapted to this music.

227. Jesus is Coming.

J. W. VAN DE VENTER.   W. C. WEEDEN.

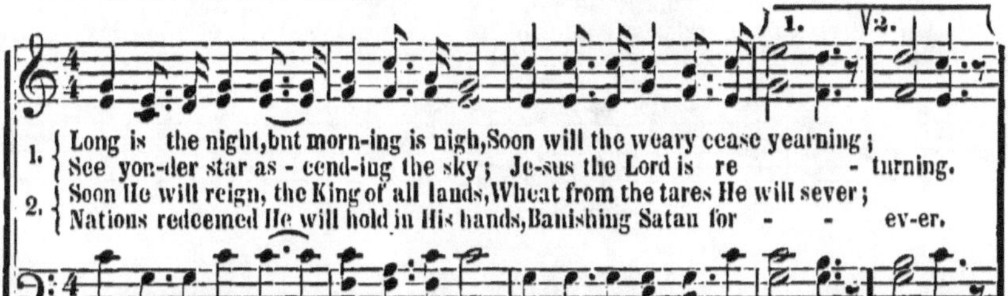

1. Long is the night, but morn-ing is nigh, Soon will the weary cease yearning;
   See yon-der star as-cend-ing the sky; Je-sus the Lord is re-turning.
2. Soon He will reign, the King of all lands, Wheat from the tares He will sever;
   Nations redeemed He will hold in His hands, Banishing Satan for-ev-er.

CHORUS.

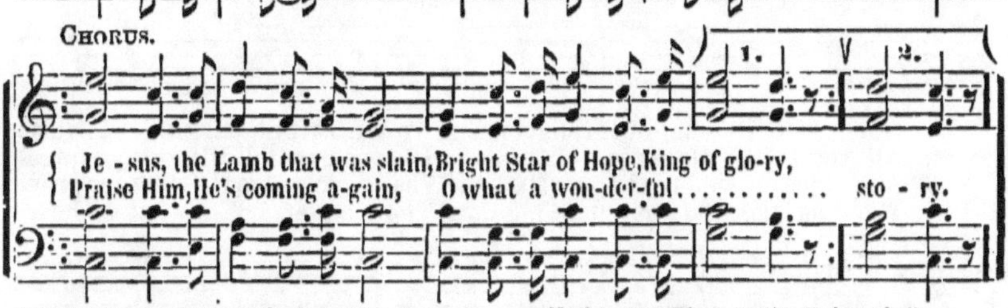

Je-sus, the Lamb that was slain, Bright Star of Hope, King of glo-ry,
Praise Him, He's coming a-gain, O what a won-der-ful .... sto-ry.

3 Watching by faith we look for the day,
   Look for eternity nearing;
   Waiting for Him, our Lord, on the way,
   Light of the world now appearing.

4 Hail to the King, to the Ruler of all,
   Coming in glory and power;
   Kingdoms of darkness before Him shall fall,
   Jesus shall reign in that hour.

Copyright, 1895, by J. W. Van De Venter and W. C. Weeden.

Needham. L. M. Concluded.

D. C. Chorus.

With all His saints I'll join to tell— My Jesus has done all things well.
But oh, His love what tongue can tell! My Jesus has done all things well.
Mercies which do all praise excel! My Jesus has done all things well.
With this I all His rage repel— My Jesus has done all things well.

A-bove the rest this note shall swell, My Jesus has done all things well.

---

230. A View of Calvary.

JOHN NEWTON.   Arr. by G. B.

This hymn was written by Rev. John Newton soon after his conversion.

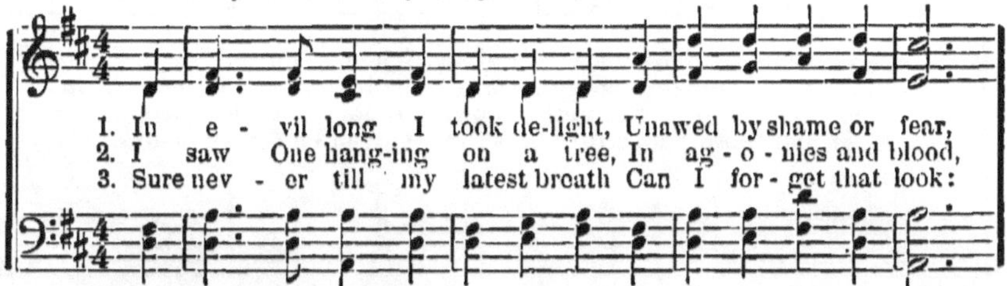

1. In evil long I took delight, Unawed by shame or fear,
2. I saw One hanging on a tree, In agonies and blood,
3. Sure never till my latest breath Can I forget that look:

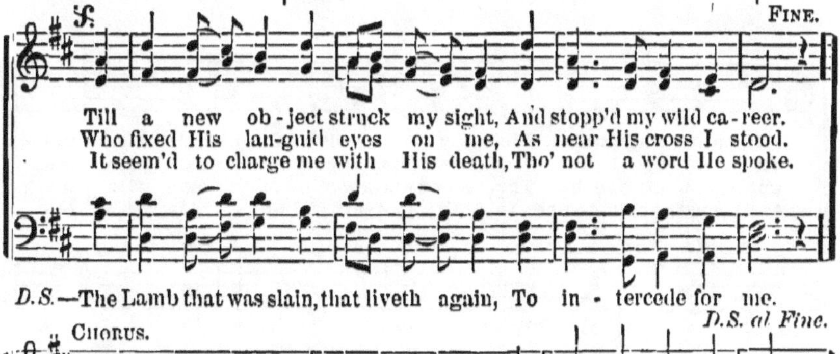

Till a new object struck my sight, And stopp'd my wild career.
Who fixed His languid eyes on me, As near His cross I stood.
It seem'd to charge me with His death, Tho' not a word He spoke.

D.S.—The Lamb that was slain, that liveth again, To intercede for me.

Chorus.

Oh, the Lamb, the bleeding Lamb, The Lamb of Calvary,

4 A second look He gave, which said,
  "I freely all forgive;
This blood is for thy ransom paid;
  I die that thou mayst live."

5 Thus, while His death my sin displays
  In all its blackest hue,
Such is the mystery of grace,
  It seals my pardon too.

Copyright, 1895, by Weeden and Weaver.

Italian Hymn. Concluded.

Help us to praise! Fa-ther all glor-i-ous, O'er all vic-tor-i-ous, Come and reign o-ver us, Ancient of Days.
Our pray'r at-tend; Come and Thy peo-ple bless, And give Thy Word suc-cess; Spir-it of ho-li-ness, On us de-scend.
In this glad hour: Thou who al-might-y art, Now rule in ev-'ry heart, And ne'er from us de-part, Spir-it of power.

233 Azmon. C. M.

ANNE STEELE.   C. G. GLASER

1. Come, you that love the Savior's name, And joy to make it known, The Sovereign of your hearts proclaim, And bow before His throne.
2. Be-hold your King, your Savior, crown'd With glories all di-vine; And tell the wond'ring nations round How bright these glories shine,
3. In-fi-nite power and boundless grace In Him u-nite their rays; You that have seen His love-ly face, Can you for-bear His praise?

4 When in the earthly courts we view
   The beauties of our King,
We long to love as angels do,
   And wish like them to sing.

5 And shall we long and wish in vain?
   Lord, teach our songs to rise!
Thy love can animate our strain,
   And bid it reach the skies.

234. Laban. C. M.

LOWELL MASON.

1. My soul, be on thy guard, Ten thousand foes a-rise;
2. Oh, watch, and fight, and pray; The bat-tle ne'er give o'er;
3. Fight on, my soul, till death Shall bring thee to thy God;

The hosts of sin are press-ing hard To draw thee from the skies,
Re-new it bold-ly ev-'ry day, And help di-vine im-plore.
He'll take thee, at thy part-ing breath, To His di-vine a-bode.

235. Fountain. C. M.

WM. COOPER.   Arr. from LOWELL MASON.

1. There is a fountain filled with blood, Drawn from Immanuel's veins,
2. The dy-ing thief rejoiced to see That fountain in his day;

And sinners, plung'd be-neath that flood, Lose all their guilt-y stains,
And there may I, tho' vile as he, Wash all my sins a-way.

FINE.

D.S.

Lose all their guilt-y stains,.... Lose all their guilt-y stains.
Wash all my sins a-way,...... Wash all my sins a-way.

3 E'er since by faith I saw the stream
   Thy flowing wounds supply,
   Redeeming love has been me theme,
   And shall be till I die.

4 And when this lisping, stammering [tongue
   Lies silent in the grave,
   Then in a nobler, sweeter song
   I'll sing Thy power to save,

236. Sitting at the Feet of Jesus. Arranged.

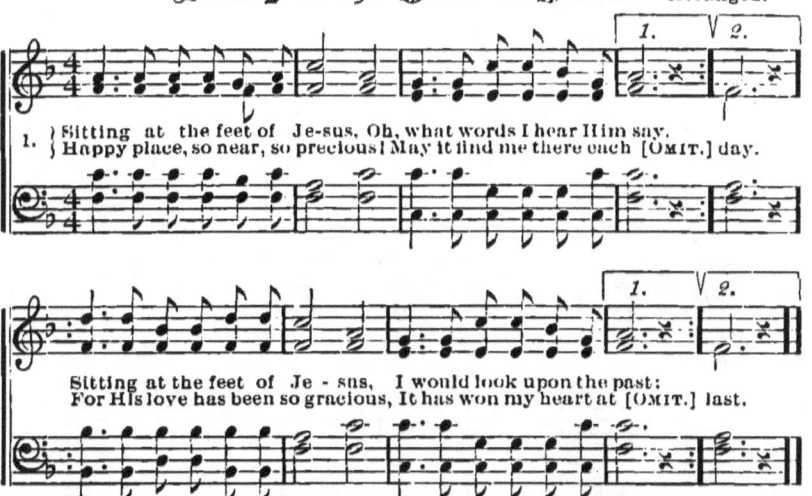

1. Sitting at the feet of Jesus, Oh, what words I hear Him say.
   Happy place, so near, so precious! May it find me there each [OMIT.] day.

Sitting at the feet of Jesus, I would look upon the past:
For His love has been so gracious, It has won my heart at [OMIT.] last.

2 Sitting at the feet of Jesus,
   Where can mortal be more blest?
 There I lay my sins and sorrows,
   And, when weary, find sweet rest;
 Sitting at the feet of Jesus,
   There I love to weep and pray
 While I from His fullness gather
   Grace and comfort every day.

3 Bless me, O my Savior, bless me,
   As I sit low at Thy feet;
 Oh, look down in love upon me,
   Let me see Thy face so sweet;
 Give me, Lord, the mind of Jesus,
   Make me holy as He is;
 May I prove I've been with Jesus,
   Who is all my righteousness.

237. Pleyel's Hymn. 7s.

T. SCOTT.   L. PLEYEL.

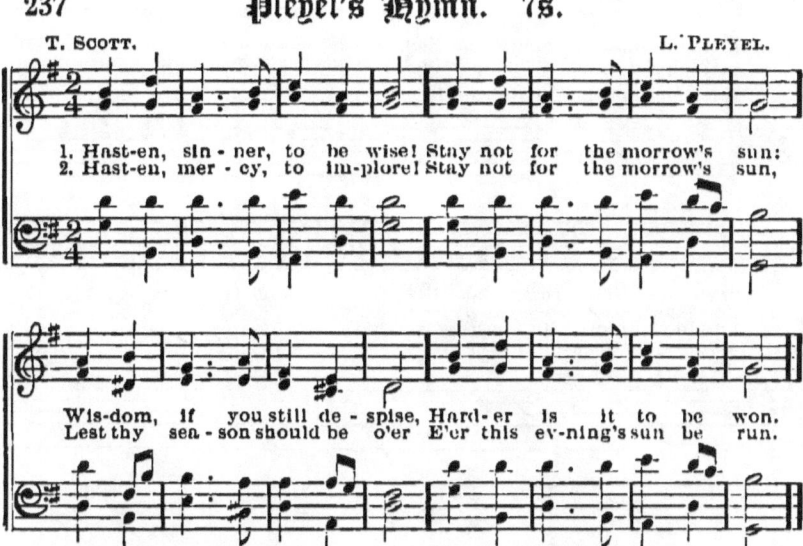

1. Hasten, sinner, to be wise! Stay not for the morrow's sun:
2. Hasten, mercy, to implore! Stay not for the morrow's sun,

Wisdom, if you still despise, Harder is it to be won.
Lest thy season should be o'er E'er this evening's sun be run.

3 Hasten, sinner, to return!
  Stay not for the morrow's sun.
  Lest thy lamp should fail to burn
  Ere salvation's work is done.

4 Hasten, sinner, to be blest!
  Stay not for the morrow's sun,
  Lest perdition thee arrest
  Ere the morrow is begun.

238. Retreat. L. M.

H. STOWELL.   THOS. HASTINGS.

1. From ev-'ry stormy wind that blows, From ev-'ry swelling tide of woes,
2. There is a place where Jesus sheds The oil of gladness on our heads—

There is a calm, a sure retreat: 'Tis found beneath the mer-cy-seat.
A place than all be-sides more sweet: It is the blood-bought mercy-seat.

3 There is a scene where spirits blend,
Where friend holds fellowship with friend;
Tho' sundered far, by faith they meet
Around one common mercy-seat.

4 O let my hand forget her skill,
My tongue be silent, cold, and still,
This bounding heart forget to beat,
Ere I forget the mercy-seat.

239. Rejoice and Be Glad.

H. BONAR.   J. J. HUSBAND.

1. Rejoice and be glad: the Redeem-er has come; Go, look on His
2. Rejoice and be glad: for the blood has been shed; Re-demption is
3. Rejoice and be glad: for the Lamb that was slain, O'er death is tri-
4. Rejoice and be glad: for He com-eth a-gain— He com-eth in

cra-dle, His cross, and His tomb. Sound His prais-es, tell the
fin-ished, the price has been paid.
umphant, and liv-eth a-gain.
glo-ry, the Lamb that was slain. Sound His prais-es, tell with

sto-ry Of Him who was slain, He liv-eth a-gain.
gladness, [OMIT.] He com-eth a-gain

3 Are there no foes for me to face?
Must I not stem the flood?
Is this vile world a friend to grace,
To help me on to God?

4 Since I must fight, if I would reign;
Increase my courage, Lord;
I'll bear the toil, endure the pain,
Supported by Thy word.

242. Lyons. 10s & 11s.

ROBERT GRANT. HAYDN.

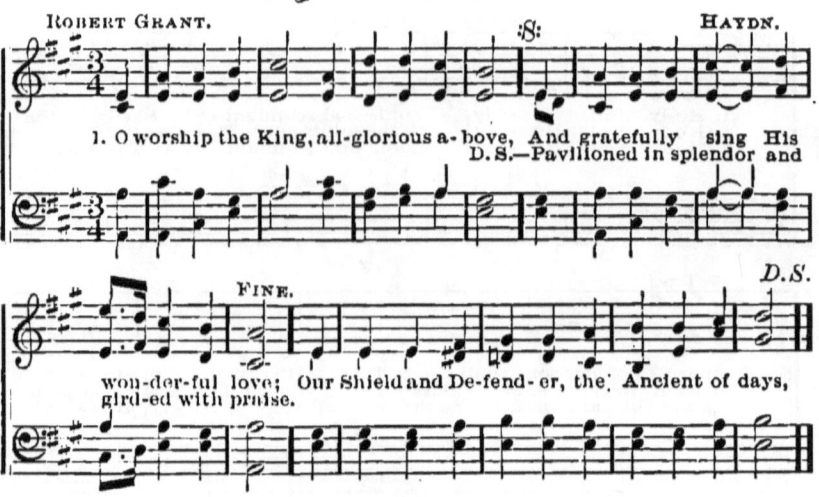

1. O worship the King, all-glorious a-bove, And gratefully sing His
   D.S.—Pavilioned in splendor and
   won-der-ful love; Our Shield and De-fend-er, the Ancient of days,
   gird-ed with praise.

2 Thy bountiful care, what tongue can recite?
  It breathes in the air, it shines in the light;
  It streams from the hills, it descends to the plain,
  And sweetly distils in the dew and the rain.

3 Frail children of dust, and feeble as frail,
  In Thee do we trust, nor find Thee to fail;
  Thy mercies, how tender! How firm to the end,
  Our Maker, Defender, Redeemer, and Friend!

4 Our Father and God, how faithful Thy love!
  While angels delight to hymn Thee above,
  The humbler creation, though feeble their lays,
  With true adoration shall lisp to Thy praise.

243. Boylston. S. M.

I. WATTS. LOWELL MASON.

1. Not all the blood of beasts, On Jew-ish al-tars slain,
2. But Christ, the heaven-ly Lamb, Bears all our sins a-way;
   Could give the guilt-y conscience peace, Or wash a-way its stain.
   A sac-ri-fice of no-bler name And rich-er blood than they.

3 My faith would lay her hand
  On that dear head of Thine,
  While, like a penitent, I stand,
  And there confess my sin.

4 Believing, we rejoice
  To see the curse remove;
  We bless the Lamb with cheerful voice,
  And sing His dying love.

244. Lenox. H. M.

C. WESLEY.   LEWIS EDSON.

1. Blow ye the trumpet, blow—The gladly solemn sound; Let all the nations know, To earth's remotest bound The year of ju-bi-lee is come: Return, ye ransom'd sinners, home, Return, ye ransom'd sin-ners, home.
2. Ex-alt the Lamb of God, The sin-a-ton-ing Lamb; Re-demption by His blood, Thro'-out the world proclaim. The year of ju-bi-lee is come: Return, ye ransom'd sinners, home, Return, ye ransom'd sin-ners, home.

3 Ye slaves of sin and hell,
  Your liberty receive,
And safe in Jesus dwell,
  And blest in Jesus live.
The year of jubilee is come:
Return, ye ransomed sinners, home.

4 Jesus, our great High Priest,
  Has full atonement made,
Ye weary spirits, rest;
  Ye mourning souls, be glad.
The year of jubilee is come:
Return, ye ransomed sinners, home.

245. St. Thomas. S. M.

WILLIAMS.

1. O come, and dwell in me. Spir-it of pow'r with-in; And bring the glor-ious lib-er-ty From sor-row, fear, and sin!
2. I want the wit-ness, Lord, That all I do is right— Ac-cord-ing to Thy will and word—Well-pleas-ing in Thy sight.
3. I ask no high-er state; in-dulge me but in this, And soon or la-ter then translate To my e-ter-nal bliss.

246. Greenville. 8s, 7s, D.

J. Newton.   J. J. Rosseau.

1. Glorious things of thee are spoken, Zi-on, city of our God;
He whose Word can not be broken, Form'd thee for His own abode.
D.C.—With salvation's wall surrounded, Thou mayest smile at all thy foes.
On the Rock of Ages founded, What can shake thy sure repose?

2 See the stream of living waters
Springing from eternal love,
Well supply thy sons and daughters,
And all fear of drought remove.
Who can faint, while such a river
Ever flows their thirst to assuage—
Grace which, like the Lord, the Giver,
Never fails from age to age?

3 Blest inhabitants of Zion,
Washed in the Redeemer's blood,
Jesus, whom their souls rely on,
Makes them kings and priests to God.

'Tis His love His people raises
With Himself to reign as kings;
And, as priests, His solemn praises,
Each for a thank-offering brings.

4 Savior, since of Zion's city
I through grace a member am,
Let the world deride or pity,
I will glory in Thy name.
Fading is the worldling's treasure,
All His boasted pomp and show;
Solid joy and lasting pleasure
None but Zion's children know.

247. Rathbun. 8s, 7s.

J. Bowring.   J. Conkey.

1. In the cross of Christ I glory, Towering o'er the wrecks of time;
2. When the woes of life o'ertake me, Hopes deceive and fears annoy,
All the light of sacred story Gathers round its head sublime.
Never shall the cross forsake me; Lo! it glows with peace and joy.

3 When the sun of bliss is beaming
Light and love upon Thy way,
From the cross the radiance streaming
Adds more luster to the day.

4 Bane and blessing, pain and pleasure,
By the cross are sanctified;
Peace is there, that knows no measure,
Joys that through all time abide.

254. The Lion of Judah.

Arr. by G. B.

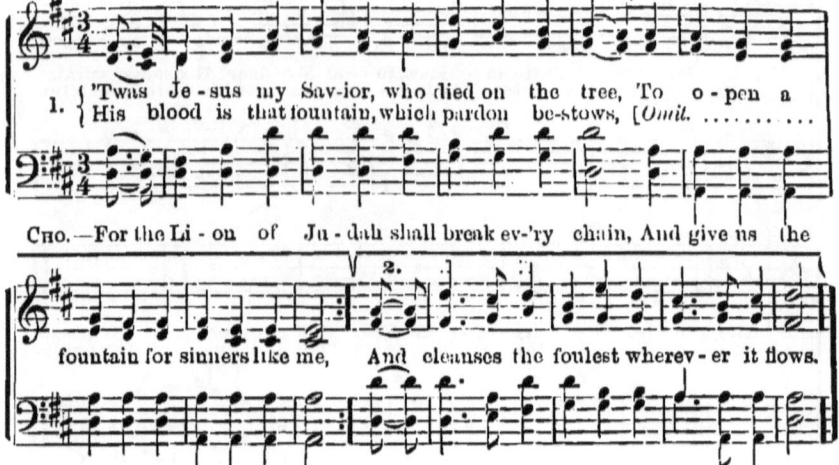

1. { 'Twas Je-sus my Sav-ior, who died on the tree, To o-pen a
   His blood is that fountain, which pardon be-stows, [Omit............

Cho.—For the Li-on of Ju-dah shall break ev-'ry chain, And give us the

fountain for sinners like me, And cleanses the foulest wherev-er it flows.

vict'ry a-gain and a-gain, And give us the vic-t'ry a-gain and a-gain

2.
And when I was willing with all things to part,
He gave me my bounty, His love in my heart;
So now I am joined with the conqering band,
Who are marching to glory at Jesus' command.

3.
Come, sinners, to Jesus, no longer delay,
A full, free salvation He offers to-day; [dream
Arouse your dark spirits, awake from your
And Jesus will save you, oh, come unto Him.

255. The Land of Canaan.

W. C. WEEDEN.

1. { There is a land of pure delight, Where saints immortal reign;
   In-finite day excludes the night, And (Omit.............. { pleasures banish pain.
2. { There everlasting spring abides, And nev-er-with'ring flowers;   ours,
   Death, like a narrow sea, divides This (Omit.............. { heav'nly land from

CHORUS.

O Canaan, bright Canaan, It is the land of Canaan, Canaan It is the land of Canaan.

3 Sweet fields beyond the swelling flood,
   Stand dressed in living green;
   So to the Jew old Canaan stood,
   While Jordan rolled between.

4 Could we but climb where Moses stood,
   And view the landscape o'er;
   Not Jordan's stream, nor death's cold flood,
   Should fright us from the shore.

Copyright, 1895, by W. C. Weeden.

258. And Shall I Turn Back.

Arr. by GRACE WEISER DAVIS.

1. My Jesus, I love Thee, I know Thou art mine, For Thee all the follies of sin I resign; My gracious Redeemer, my Savior art Thou; If ever I loved Thee, my Jesus, 'tis now.

2. I love Thee because Thou hast first loved me, And purchased my pardon on Calvary's tree; I love Thee for wearing the thorns on Thy brow; If ever I loved Thee, my Jesus, 'tis now.

3. I'll love Thee in life, I will love Thee in death, And praise Thee as long as Thou giv'st me breath, And say when the death-dew lies cold on my brow: If ever I loved Thee, my Jesus, 'tis now.

4. In mansions of glory and endless delight, I'll ever adore Thee in heaven so bright; I'll sing with the glittering crown on my brow, If ever I loved Thee, my Jesus, 'tis now.

CHORUS.

And shall I turn back into the world? O, no, not I, not I! And shall I turn back into the world? No, no, not I!
I'll never turn back, never turn back, O, no, not I, not I! I'll never turn back, never turn back, O, no, not I!

Copyright, 1894, by Grace Weiser Davis. Used by per.

The Lily of the Valley.

Arr. by Joshua Gill.

1. I've found a friend in Jesus, He's everything to me, He's the fair-est of ten thousand to my soul; The Li-ly of the Valley in Him a-lone I see, All I need to cleanse and make me fully whole. In sorrow He's my comfort, in trouble He's my stay, He tells me ev-'ry care on Him to roll. He's the Lily of the Val-ley, the bright and morning Star, He's the fairest of ten thousand to my soul.

2. He all my griefs has taken, and all my sorrows borne; In temp-ta-tion He's my strong and mighty tow'r; I've all for Him forsaken, I've all my idols torn From my heart, and now He keeps me by His pow'r. Tho' all the world forsake me, and Satan tempts me sore, Thro' Je-sus I shall safe-ly reach the goal. He's the Lily of the

3. He'll never, never leave me, nor yet forsake me here, While I live by faith and do His blessed will; A wall of fire about me, I've nothing now to fear: With His man-na He my hun-gry soul shall fill; Then sweeping up to glory we see His blessed face, Where riv-ers of de-light shall ev-er roll. He's the Lily of the

Chorus.—In sorrow He's my comfort, in trouble He's my stay, He tells me ev-'ry care on Him to roll. He's the Lily of the

Hallelujah!

D.S.

Valley, the bright and morning Star, He's the fairest of ten thousand to my soul.

Copyright, 1884, by McDonald & Gill.

260 I Love to Sing those Songs of Old.

"Thus saith the Lord, Stand ye in the ways, and see, and ask for the old paths where is the good way and walk therein."—Jer. vi: 16.

MARY IRENE McLEAN. TO MARION LAWRANCE. A. F. MYERS. By per.

Moderato.

1. I love to sing the songs of old, To me they are so dear,
2. When waves of an-guish o'er me roll, A re-fuge blest are they,
3. And when I sing my ti-tle clear, "To mansions in the skies,"
4. My heart is cheered when e'er I hear, "Blest be the tie that binds,"
5. When "Watchmen tell us of the night,"My wait-ing spir-it sings.
6. Sweet fields be-yond the swell-ing flood, Seems near-er day by day,
7. I hope the friends who round me weep, Will sing when death is near,
8. "All hail the pow'r of Je-sus' name," Tri-um-phant sings my soul,

They keep my heart from grow-ing cold, They calm my ev-'ry fear.
And "Je-sus, Lov-er of my Soul," Soothes all my pain a-way.
My sor-est trou-bles dis-ap-pear, As mist from sun-shine flies.
For love makes fel-low-ship so dear, U-ni-ting Christian minds.
A rain-bow prom-ise greets my sight, And rap-ture with it brings.
E'er since my Sav-ior's cleansing blood, Washed all my guilt a-way.
"A-sleep in Je-sus, bless-ed sleep," To rob the grave of fear.
Be-fore His throne I'll sing the strains, While count-less a-ges roll.

CHORUS.

I love those songs, those pre-cious songs of old,
love to sing those songs of old,

those songs, those songs, I love those songs of old.
songs of old, those songs of old,

First and last stanzas and Chorus by A. F. M.

261. My Jesus, I Love Thee.

London Hymn Book.   A. J. Gordon.

1. My Jesus, I love Thee, I know Thou art mine, For Thee all the follies of sin I resign; My gracious Redeemer, my Saviour art Thou, If ever I loved Thee, my Jesus, 'tis now.
2. I love Thee, because Thou hast first loved me, And purchased my pardon on Calvary's tree; I love Thee for wearing the thorns on Thy brow; If ever I loved Thee, my Jesus, 'tis now.
3. I will love Thee in life, I will love Thee in death, And praise Thee as long as Thou lendest me breath; And say when the death-dew lies cold on my brow; If ever I loved Thee, my Jesus, 'tis now.
4. In mansions of glory and endless delight, I'll ever adore Thee in heaven so bright; I'll sing with the glittering crown on my brow; If ever I loved Thee, my Jesus, 'tis now.

By permission.

262. Come, Ye Disconsolate.

T. Moore.   11, 10.

1. Come, ye disconsolate, where'er ye languish, Come to the mercy-seat, fervently kneel; Here bring your wounded hearts, here tell your anguish; Earth has no sorrow that Heav'n cannot heal.

2 Joy of the desolate, light of the straying,
   Hope of the penitent, fadeless and pure,
Here speaks the Comforter, tenderly saying,
   "Earth has no sorrow that Heaven cannot cure."

3 Here see the bread of life; see waters flowing
   Forth from the throne of God, pure from above;
Come to the feast of love; come, ever knowing
   Earth has no sorrow but heaven can remove.

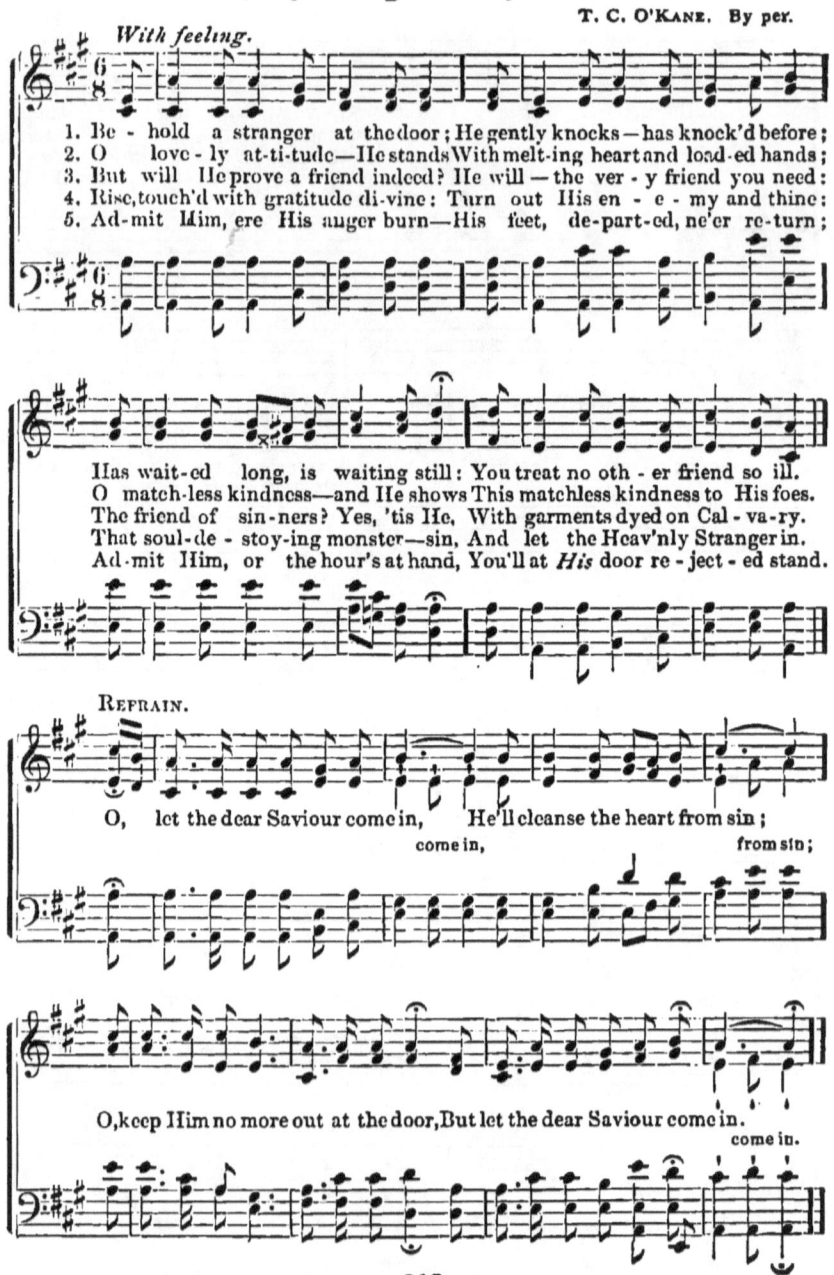

5 His only righteousness I show.
His saving truth proclaim;
'Tis all my business here below
To cry, Behold the Lamb!

6 Happy, if with my latest breath
I may but gasp His name:
Preach Him to all, and cry in death,
Behold, behold the Lamb!

267. Behold, the Bridegroom Comes.

J. M. W.
J. M. WHYTE.

1. We shall hear a voice, an im-mor-tal voice, "Behold, the Bridegroom comes!" At the mid-night watch, in the dark-ness deep, When a-cross our souls heav-y slum-bers creep, We shall hear that voice, that im-mor-tal voice, "Be-hold, the Bridegroom comes!"
2. When the voice shall cry, "Go ye forth to-night, Behold, the Bridegroom comes!" Then the pulse will cease, and the heart grow still, And the eyes will close, and the blood grow chill, And the soul will take its e-ter-nal flight, "For lo, the Bridegroom comes!"
3. Brother, trim your lamp, have it burning bright "Behold, the Bridegroom comes!" He will sure-ly come, though he seem-eth late, Be at peace with him, nor a mo-ment wait, You will hear the cry ere the morning light, "Behold, the Bridegroom comes!"
4. Hast thou made a vow? has-ten ye to pay, "Behold, the Bridegroom comes!" For when he has come, and hath closed the door, And ye stand and pray, "O-pen, we im-plore," It will be too late,—pay thy vows to-day, "Behold, the Bridegroom comes!"

CHORUS.

O be read-y when the Bridegroom comes! O be read-y when the

Copyright, 1890, by R. R. McCabe & Co. By permission.

Behold, the Bridegroom Comes. Concluded.

268   **Marching to Glory.**
Tune—Marching Through Georgia.
Key of B Flat.

1 Come with hearts and voices now and sing a gospel song,
Sing it with a spirit that will move the mighty throng;
Sing it till the world shall hear the echoes loud and long,
    While we are marching to glory.
Cho.—Then hail! all hail! the coming jubilee!
    Redeemed from sin, our Jesus make us free;
    Now we'll shout salvation over mountain land and sea,
    While we are marching to glory!

2 Gird the gospel armor on and duty's call obey;
See the host of Satan ready marshaled for the fray;
Going forth to meet them we will watch and fight and pray,
    While we are marching to glory!

3 Forward then to battle 'neath the banner of the cross;
Counting worldly honors at their best as only dross;
Jesus is our Captain, and we ne'er can suffer loss,
    While we are marching to glory!

272   *O Sabbath! 'tis of Thee.*
TUNE—"America." Key G.

1 O SABBATH! 'tis of thee,
   Sweet day of liberty
     And worshiping;
   Type of the soul's repose,
   Day when my Lord arose,
   Blest at creation's close,
     Of thee I sing.

2 Thou treasure-house of pray'r,
   Thou balm for pain and care,
     Thou fount of praise;
   Thy mornings breathe release,
   Thy evenings whisper peace,
   Thy anthems never cease,
     Thou psalm of days.

3 Forth on thy wings of white,
   Plumed in celestial light,
     Sweet Sabbath Day;
   Fly all the earth abroad,
   Till all thy beauty laud,
   Till all adore thy God;
     All hope, all pray.

4 Our fathers' God, to Thee,
   Author of Sanctity,
     To Thee we sing;
   May all the world revere
   This day so old, so dear;
   O, bring Thy presence near,
     Great God our King.
            Rev. HENRY OSTROM.

273   *My Faith Looks up to Thee.*
Music page 80.

1 MY faith looks up to Thee,
   Thou Lamb of Calvary,
     Savior divine:
   Now hear me while I pray,
   Take all my guilt away;
   Oh, let me from this day
     Be wholly Thine.

2 May Thy rich grace impart
   Strength to my fainting heart,
     My zeal inspire;
   As Thou hast died for me,
   Oh, may my love to Thee
   Pure, warm, and changeless be,—
     A living fire.

3 When ends life's transient dream,
   When death's cold, sullen stream
     Shall o'er me roll;
   Blest Savior, then, in love,
   Fear and distress remove;
   Oh, bear me safe above,—
     A ransomed soul.

274   *O Happy Day.* Music page 80.

1 O HAPPY day that fix'd my choice
   On Thee, my Savior and my God!
   Well may my glowing heart rejoice,
   And tell its raptures all abroad.

CHO.—Happy day, happy day,
   When Jesus washed my sins away!
   He taught me how to watch and pray,
   And live rejoicing every day, etc.

2 O happy bond, that seals my vows
   To Him who merits all my love!
   Let cheerful anthems fill His house,
   While to that sacred shrine I move.

3 'Tis done! the great transaction's done!
   I am my Lord's, and He is mine;
   He drew me, and I followed on,
   Charmed to confess the voice divine,

4 Now rest, my long-divided heart;
   Fix'd on this blissful center, rest;
   Nor ever from thy Lord depart;
   With Him of every good possess'd.

275   *There is a Happy Land.* Music page 81.

1 THERE is a happy land,
     Far, far away;
   Where saints in glory stand,
     Bright, bright as day;
   Oh, how they sweetly sing,
   Worthy is the Savior King,
   Loud let His praises ring,
     Praise, praise for aye.

2 Come to that happy land,
     Come, come away;
   Why will ye doubting stand,
     Why still delay?
   Oh, we shall happy be,
   When, from sin and sorrow free,
   Lord, we shall live with Thee,
     Blest, blest for aye.

3 Bright is that happy land,
     Beams every eye;
   Kept by a Father's hand,
     Love cannot die.
   Oh, then, to glory run,
   Be a crown and kingdom won,
   And bright above the sun
     We'll reign for aye.

276   *All Hail the Power of Jesus' Name!*
Music page 81.

1 ALL hail the power of Jesus' name!
   Let angels prostrate fall;
   Bring forth the royal diadem,
   And crown Him Lord of all.

2 Sinners, whose love can ne'er forget
   The wormwood and the gall,
   Go, spread your trophies at His feet,
   And crown Him Lord of all.

3 Let every kindred, every tribe,
   On this terrestrial ball,
   To Him all majesty ascribe,
   And crown Him Lord of all.

4 O that with yonder sacred throng
   We at His feet may fall!
   We'll join the everlasting song,
   And crown Him Lord of all.

INDEX.

First lines in roman ; Titles in CAPITALS ; Metrical Tunes in *italic*.

	No.
Abide with me, fast falls the eventide,	231
A HAPPY BAND ARE WE,	105
A home on high is waiting me,	150
Alas ! and did my Savior bleed?,	15
Aldene. S. M.,	150
A LITTLE WHILE WITH JESUS,	164
All hail the power of Jesus' name,	276
All my doubts I give to Jesus,	41
ALL THE WAY TO CALVARY,	151
ALWAYS WITH US,	43
Amazing grace, how sweet the sound,	85
AMERICA ! LAND OF THE FREE,	189
Am I a soldier of the cross,	241
AND SHALL I TURN BACK,	258
ANGELS HOV'RING ROUND,	217
Antioch. C. M.,	250
AN UNDIVIDED HEART FOR CHRIST,	66
ARE YOU WALKING IN THE LIGHT,	206
ARE YOU WASHED IN THE BLOOD ?,	67
Are you weary, are you heavy-hearted,	75
Arlington. C. M.,	241
A SHELTER IN THE TIME OF STORM,	101
A sinner was wand'ring at eventide,	190
AT THE CROSS,	256
AT THE CROSS I'LL ABIDE,	89
AT THE FOUNTAIN,	163
At the sounding of the trumpet, when the sa	64
A VIEW OF CALVARY,	230
Aron. C. M.,	169
Azmon. C. M.,	233
BE A GOLDEN SUNBEAM,	22
BE NOT AFRAID,	182
Behold a Stranger at the door,	265
Behold, behold the Lamb of God,	13
BEHOLD, THE BRIDEGROOM COMES,	267
BELIEVE AND BE SAVED,	185
BEYOND DEATH'S SILENT RIVER,	124
BEYOND THE SWELLING FLOOD,	168
BLESSED ASSURANCE,	138
BLESSED BE HIS NAME,	119
BLESSED BE THE NAME,	111
BLESS ME NOW,	220
BLIND BARTIMEUS,	117
Blissful hours when first I knew Him,	11
Blow ye the trumpet, blow,	244
Boyleston. S. M.,	243
BRINGING IN THE SHEAVES,	33
BRINGING THE WORLD TO JESUS,	24
BUILDING DAY BY DAY,	208
By faith I see my Savior dying,	17
CALVARY,	127
Can it be that Jesus bought me,	48
CHEER FOR THE THIRSTY,	102
Christian, be faithful, follow me closely,	60
CHRIST VICTORIOUS,	77
Cling to the Mighty One,	171
COME AWAY TO JESUS NOW,	71
COME CLOSE TO THE SAVIOR,	94
Come, Holy Spirit, heavenly Dove,	225
COME, OH, COME,	74
COME, SAINTS, AND ADORE HIM,	98
Come, sing again the song of love,	173
Come, sinner, behold what Jesus hath done,	120
COME, SINNER, COME,	149
Come, sinners, to the gospel feast,	131
Come, Thou almighty King,	232
COME TO THE SAVIOR, COME,	131
Come, trembling sinner, in whose breast,	72
COME UNTO ME,	112
Come weal, come woe, where'er we go,	182
Come, weep just as we did in sorrow for sin,	71
Come with hearts and voices now and sing a	208
COME, YE DISCONSOLATE,	262
Come, ye sinners, poor and needy,	199
Come, you that love the Savior's name,	233
CONSECRATION,	123
CORONATION,	81

	No.
CROWN HIM,	106
DARE TO SAY NO,	152
Dear Lord, increase my faith, I pray,	211
Don't you hear the cry of the tempest toss'd,	134
Down at the cross the Savior found me,	34
DOWN IN THE LICENSED SALOON,	136
Doxology. L. M.,	133
DO YOU KNOW THE SONG ?,	16
Draw near, O Christ, to me,	161
Duane Street. L. M. D.,	183
Each cooing dove, and sighing bough,	139
Earth's physicians know not to heal thee,	29
Eventide. 10s,	231
FALL INTO LINE, BOYS,	78
Fall in ! ye soldiers of the Lord,	196
FAREWELL,	209
Fear not, little flock, says the Savior divine,	20
FOLLOW ALL THE WAY,	155
For the blessed source of truth,	50
FOR THESE MY SOUL IS LOST,	132
FOR YOU AND FOR ME,	6
Fountain. C. M.,	235
From Egypt's cruel bondage fled,	107
From ev'ry danger, doubt and fear,	76
From ev'ry stormy wind that blows,	238
Glorious things of thee are spoken,	246
GLORY TO GOD, HALLELUJAH,	210
GLORY TO THE BLEEDING LAMB,	173
"Go bring me," said the dying fair,	132
God always deals in love,	159
GOD BE WITH YOU,	167
GOD IS ABLE TO DELIVER THEE,	76
Good resolves won't save me,	53
GOOD-NIGHT,	169
Greenville. 8s, 7s, D.,	246
HALLELUJAH TO THE LAMB,	175
Hark ! I hear a soft refrain,	80
Hark ! I hear a warning voice,	135
HARK ! TEN THOUSAND HARPS,	207
Hark, the voice of Jesus calling,	70
Harwell. 8s & 7s, 8 lines,	207
Hasten, sinner, to be wise,	237
Have you been to Jesus for the cleansing p	6
Have you ever heard the story,	140
Have you had a kindness shown,	100
HEAVEN IS MY HOME,	226
He hath spoken, "Be still," the Rebuker of	3
HE IS CALLING,	141
Help us, O Lord, Thy yoke to wear,	249
HE SAVES TO THE UTTERMOST,	73
HE SOUGHT AND FOUND ME,	45
HE'S THE PRINCE OF PEACEMAKERS,	3
Holy, holy, holy ! Lord God Almighty,	240
HOLY SPIRIT FROM ABOVE,	10
How sweet the name of Jesus sounds,	111
HOW THEY CRUCIFIED MY LORD,	25
I am bound for the land of the living God,	143
I am going up, dear Papa,	187
I AM RESTING IN THE SAVIOR'S LOVE,	271
I AM SAVED IN JESUS,	53
"I am the way," the Savior said,	203
I AM TRUSTING,	41
I AM TRUSTING IN MY SAVIOR,	205
I BRING MY ALL TO THEE,	257
I brought my sins to Calvary,	213
I can hear my Savior calling,	155
I CAN, I WILL, I DO BELIEVE,	165
I follow the footsteps of Jesus, my Lord,	103
If the name of the Savior is precious to you,	40
If you will, you may know the gladness of y	148
I go forth to-day on my pilgrim way,	223
I have a Shepherd, one I love so well,	68
I have found a Friend, oh, such a Friend,	175
I HAVE FOUND JESUS,	37
I have found the great salvation,	119
I HAVE IT IN MY SOUL, HALLELUJAH,	179
I have precious news to tell,	18

INDEX.

Title	No.
I HAVE REDEEMED THEE,	69
I hear the heavenly bells to-night,	63
I'LL GO TO JESUS,	72
I'll sing of the story,	192
I'LL WORK FOR JESUS,	23
I love to meditate, O God,	270
I LOVE TO SING THOSE SONGS OF OLD,	260
I'm a pilgrim bound for glory,	37
I'm but a stranger here,	226
I'M GLAD SALVATION'S FREE,	224
I'M GOING HOME TO GLORY,	204
I'm kneeling at the mercy seat,	165
I'M NOT AFRAID,	57
I MUST TELL JESUS,	137
I NEED THEE, LORD,	145
In a world of sorrow,	110
In evil long I took delight,	230
In the Cross of Christ I glory,	247
In the Master's vineyard labor day by day,	26
In the precious Bible,	59
In this world, where shadows,	193
In vain in high and holy lays,	147
I once was on the road to woe,	47
IS IT FOR ME,	44
IS IT NOTHING TO YOU,	31
I stand; but not as once I did,	176
Is there a sinner awaiting,	202
Italian Hymn,	232
I TELL HIM ALL,	9
IT WAS FOR ME,	38
I've found a Friend in Jesus,	259
Jesus, and didst Thou leave the sky,	170
JESU! DIDS YOU COME,	55
Jesus hath died and hath risen again,	113
JESUS IS CALLING NOW,	51
Jesus is calling, tenderly calling,	104
JESUS IS CALLING TO-DAY,	195
JESUS IS COMING,	227
JESUS IS MINE,	63
JESUS IS PASSING THIS WAY,	202
Jesus is pleading with my poor soul,	180
JESUS LEADS THE WAY,	21
JESUS LIVES,	126
Jesus my all to heaven is gone,	133
JESUS, MY SAVIOR,	36
Jesus of Nazareth,	212
JESUS SAVES ME NOW,	113
Jesus, see me at Thy feet,	91
Jesus, take this heart of stone,	220
JESUS TENDERLY CALLING,	104
Jesus, the name high over all,	266
JESUS, WE ARE COMING,	59
Joy to the world! the Lord is come,	250
Just as thou art, without one trace,	74
JUST THE SAME TO-DAY,	140
KEEP MOVING ON THE WAY,	154
Laban. C.M.,	234
LEAD ME, SAVIOR,	121
LEANING ON THE EVERLASTING ARMS,	166
Lenox. H.M.,	244
LESS OF SELF,	115
LET IT FALL,	225
Lift up your heads, ye pilgrims,	4
LISTEN TO MY STORY,	34
LITTLE THINGS,	58
Long is the night, but morning is nigh,	227
Lord of the living harvest,	69
Lord, Thou hast in this wide world,	222
Lord, we come before Thee now,	253
Lyons. 10s & 11s,	242
MAKE ROOM FOR JESUS,	61
Manoah. S.M.,	249
MARCHING TO CANAAN,	177
MARCHING TO GLORY,	268
MARCH ON,	142
MASTER, USE ME,	19
May fainting souls approach the Lord,	102
MEMORIES OF GALILEE,	130
MERCY AT THE CROSS,	128
MERCY'S FREE,	17
Mighty army of the young,	126
MIGHTY TO SAVE,	144
My body, soul and spirit,	123
My brother, the glad gospel message I bring,	49
My faith looks up to Thee,	273
My heart is full of gladness,	204
MY HEART'S PRAYER,	211
My Jesus, I love Thee,	258, 261
MY MOTHER'S HANDS,	181
My Savior died upon the tree,	218
"My son, give me thy heart," I hear the Sav	66
My soul, be on thy guard,	234
MY SPIRIT IS FREE,	103
NEARER TO ME,	161
Needham. L.M.,	229
Nicea. 12, 10,	240
Not all the blood of beasts,	243
Not all the gold of all the world,	12
NOTHING BUT THE BLOOD OF JESUS,	65
NOTHING BUT THY BLOOD,	91
Now in a song of grateful praise,	229
O beautiful day, bright Sabbath day,	186
O brother, are you ready should the	5
O child of God, awake, awake from sleeping,	7
O come, and dwell in me,	245
Of Him who did salvation bring,	163
O, for a thousand tongues to sing,	252
O happy day that fixed my choice,	274
Oh, come, believe on Jesus,	54
Oh, guilty sinner! to-day begin,	185
Oh, how dark the night that wrapt my spirit	151
OH, HOW I LOVE JESUS. C.M.,	260
OH, IT IS WONDERFUL,	48
Oh, my heart is thrilled with wondrous joy	271
Oh, now I see the crimson wave,	122
Oh, scatter seeds of loving deeds,	194
Oh, the gospel story tell,	42
Oh, those beautiful, beautiful hands,	181
OH, WANDERER LOST,	269
Oh, why thus stand with reluctant feet,	71
O, I NEVER CAN FORGET,	52
O Jesus, Lord, Thy dying love,	236
O Jesus, Savior, I long to rest,	89
O land of rest, for thee I sigh,	219
O list the voice of Jesus say,	112
O, love surpassing knowledge,	35
O mourner in Zion, how blessed art thou,	79
ON CALVARY THERE STOOD A CROSS,	87
ONE BY ONE WE'LL ALL BE GATHERED,	263
ONE SOUL FOR JESUS,	7
ONLY TOUCH HIM,	29
On the brow of night there shines a silver star	56
ON THE CROSS,	13
On the cross of Calvary Jesus died for you	38
On the mountain's top appearing,	248
ONWARD UP THE HIGHWAY,	96
O Sabbath! 'tis of thee,	272
O sinner, take heed when scattering seed,	116
O, THOSE BLISSFUL HOURS,	11
Our blessed Redeemer came down from above	73
OUR COUNTRY'S VOICE,	162
Our Father, who art in heaven,	83
Our sighs and tears,	57
OUR TRUE FRIEND,	108
Out in the streets and by-ways,	24
OVER THE BORDER LAND,	150
O worship the King, all-glorious above,	242
PAPA, SHALL I LOOK FOR YOU,	187
PASS IT ON,	100
Pleyel's Hymn. 7s,	237
Praise God from whom all blessings flow,	133
Praise ye the Lord, joyfully shout hosanna,	172
Precious Savior, we are Thine,	100
PRECIOUS TRUTH,	50
PREPARE TO MEET THY GOD,	135
RAISE THE SONG TRIUMPHANT,	200
Rathbun. 8s, 7s,	247
REDEEMER OF ZION,	28
REJOICE AND BE GLAD,	239
Retreat. L.M.,	238
Rockingham. L.M.,	95
Rose of Sharon, thy rich fragrance,	30

INDEX.

Title	No.
Sabbath day song,	186
Salvation through the blood,	12
Saved by His blood,	46
Savior, is there anything,	221
Savior, keep me near thee,	86
Savior, lead me, lest I stray,	121
Savior, make me pure within,	86
Scattering precious seed,	93
Scatter the flowers,	26
Seeds of promise,	194
Send me forth, O blessed Master,	19
Send the light,	130
Send us out as gleaners,	69
Shall I be saved to-night?,	180
Sing, all ye ransomed of the Lord,	142
Sing on,	158
Sinners, turn; why will ye die,	251
Sitting at the feet of Jesus,	236
Softly and tenderly Jesus is calling,	6
Soldiers of the Lord,	90
Sometime,	178
Songs that mother sang,	80
Sought and found,	14
Sowing in the morning,	33
Sowing the tares,	188
Standing by the cross,	156
Steadily marching on,	172
Step out on the promise,	79
St. Martin's. C.M.,	252
Story of the cross,	42
St. Thomas. S.M.,	245
Sunshine of love,	193
Sweet are the promises,	39
Sweetly comes the holy greeting,	84
Sweet Rose of Sharon,	30
Sweet the moments rich in blessing,	156
Sweet words of peace,	183
Take hold of the life-line,	49
Tell it to-day,	40
Tell it to Jesus,	75
That's enough for me,	35
The Believer's Standing,	176
The Bleeding Lamb,	218
The Bridegroom cometh,	5
The Cleansing Wave,	122
The day of jubilee,	196
The deed was done, the debt was paid,	114
The fountain,	157
The fountain now is open,	199
The grace of God,	32
The haven,	129
The King's highway,	125
The land of Canaan,	255
The Lily of the Valley,	259
The Lion of Judah,	254
The Lord is my Shepherd,	68
The Lord's Prayer,	83
The lost soul's lament,	214
The Master is calling,	70
The morning cometh,	4
The New Jerusalem,	143
The open tomb,	114
The Pharisee and Publican,	82
The prize is set before us,	62
The Savior called so lovingly,	46
The Savior found me dying,	45
The Savior sought and found me,	14
The silver star,	56
The sinner and the song,	190
The soul who would find full release from h	61
The Stranger at the door,	265
The summer is ended, O God,	214
The time for parting now has come,	169
The way, the truth, the life,	203
There are angels hov'ring 'round,	217
There is a dear and hallowed spot,	127
There is a fountain filled with blood,	157, 235
There is a green hill far away,	27
There is a happy land,	275
There is a land of pure delight,	255
There is only one thing that the Christian n	154
There's a call comes ringing o'er the restless	130
There's a haven safely locked,	129
There's a wideness in God's mercy,	141
There went to the temple to offer up prayer,	82
They are covered by the blood,	213
They crucified Him,	120
Thou sweet smiling Kedron, by the silver st	98
Throw out the line,	134
Thy grace, O my Savior,	32
'Tis my all,	221
'Tis sweet to lean on Jesus' breast,	21
To-day the Savior calls,	228
To save a poor sinner,	192
Triumph by and by,	62
Trusting in His faithfulness,	223
Trying to shine for Jesus,	110
'Twas Jesus my Savior, who died on the tree,	254
Waiting by the open door,	84
Waiting is the golden harvest,	264
Wait! wait! Jesus will come,	174
Walking daily with the Master,	77
Wake the strain, the glad refrain,	105
Wash my sins away,	47
Was it for me that Jesus died,	44
Watch ye and wait, O brethren of God,	174
We are building in sorrow, and building in j	208
We are never, never weary of the grand old	210
We are soldiers of the cross,	216
We are soldiers true and valiant in the army	90
We are Thine,	109
We are trav'ling to a better land,	263
Weeden. C.M.,	270
We have a Friend who loves us well,	108
We have a rock, a safe retreat,	101
Welcome evening shadows,	215
We'll never say good-bye,	118
We'll work till Jesus comes,	219
We praise Thee, O Lord,	97
We're bound for the land of the pure and the	92
We're marching to Mount Zion,	125
We're on the way to Canaan's land,	107
We shall hear a voice, an immortal voice,	267
We shall stand before the King,	146
We've enlisted in the army of the Lord,	78
We will sing the praise of Jesus,	160
What a fellowship, what a joy divine,	166
What a gath'ring that will be,	64
What can wash away my sin,	65
Whatever you sow you must reap,	116
What I have written,	212
What various hindrances we meet,	95
What will you do with Jesus,	8
What work hast thou for me?,	222
Whence Jesus came I cannot tell,	117
When cherished joys have taken wing,	145
When I think how they crucified my Lord,	25
When the roll is called up yonder,	198
When the trumpet of the Lord shall sound,	198
When we all get home,	160
When you see a mighty forest,	58
Where He leads I'll follow,	39
Where is my wand'ring boy to-night,	136
While Jesus whispers to you,	149
Whiter than the snow,	20
Who is ready?,	264
Will you go?,	92
With joy we are marching to Zion's bright	177
Wonderful is the Savior,	184
Wonderful love,	170
Wonderful love of Jesus,	147
Wonderful story of love,	88
Wondrously redeemed,	18
Yes, the sorrow, pain and woe,	118
Yes, we're coming,	54
Yes, we shall meet beyond the flood,	108
Yield not to temptation,	99
You may, if you will,	148
Zion. 8s, 7s & 4s,	248

TOPICAL INDEX.

Acceptance.—17, 68, 103, 119, 165.

Activity.—7, 22, 26, 61, 77, 78, 90, 96, 97, 125, 142, 154, 172, 182, 216, 264.

Atonement.—12, 13, 15, 25, 27, 38, 87, 114, 120, 151, 218, 230, 235.

Believe.—79, 179, 185.

Calling.—45, 51, 70, 104, 141, 155, 180, 195, 228.

Christmas.—16, 56, 140, 207, 250.

Closing Service—64, 133, 167, 169, 209, 215, 231.

Consecration.—66, 91, 109, 115, 123, 157, 163, 219, 220, 221, 257.

Cross.—38, 42, 44, 89, 128, 247, 256.

Encouragement.—4, 5, 20, 60, 62, 143, 146, 182, 206, 227, 248.

Faith.—9, 171, 174, 198, 204, 208, 210, 217.

Fellowship.—11, 43, 44, 94, 137.

Gospel.—140, 212, 243, 248.

Grace.—32, 85, 183.

Gratitude.—21, 40, 48, 52, 63, 98, 103, 113, 173, 184, 213, 236.

Guidance.—28, 99, 121, 232.

Heaven.—64, 118, 124, 150, 160, 168, 178, 198, 204, 226, 255, 263.

Holy Spirit.—10, 225.

Invitation.—6, 8, 49, 55, 61, 67, 71, 72, 73, 74, 75, 84, 92, 112, 131, 149, 185, 195, 199, 202, 203, 228, 233, 243, 251, 262, 265, 269, 275, 276.

Jesus.—24, 36, 53, 61, 106, 111, 113, 137, 164, 202, 227, 236, 254, 258, 259, 261, 266.

Joy.—18, 22, 184, 193, 239, 252.

Love.—14, 15, 88, 147, 170.

Missionary.—130, 134, 162.

Obedience.—19, 23, 39, 54, 59, 68, 72.

Peace.—3, 183.

Praise.—34, 35, 37, 43, 46, 47, 97, 103, 111, 117, 119, 133, 138, 158, 192, 200, 210, 224, 229, 233, 240, 243, 250, 259, 266, 272, 274, 276.

Prayer.—36, 83, 95, 145, 179, 211, 249, 253, 273.

Promise.—140, 174, 185, 203, 235.

Protection.—76, 86, 101, 108, 129, 189.

Purity.—208, 211, 235, 245.

Rallying.—96, 100, 105, 107, 142, 177, 196, 216.

Refuge.—57, 139, 161, 238.

Resting.—109, 122, 127, 138, 163, 165, 166, 196, 258, 261, 271.

Salvation.—29, 46, 47, 65, 67, 73, 224, 244.

Sinner.—71, 149, 190, 251, 265.

Solos.—80, 82, 116, 117, 120, 132, 180, 181, 187, 188, 190, 205, 214, 260.

Sowing.—69, 93, 116, 188, 194.

Sunday School.—50, 58, 59, 60, 62, 69, 78, 88, 93, 94, 96, 97, 100, 105, 106, 108, 110, 112, 121, 125, 126, 131, 139, 140, 146, 148, 151, 154, 158, 166, 170, 172, 173, 174, 182, 184, 186, 192, 193, 194, 196, 198, 200, 208, 210, 213, 216.

Supplication.—19, 36, 47, 69, 86, 121, 145, 211, 221, 245, 249, 253, 270, 273.

Temperance.—31, 134, 152.

Trial.—159, 187.

Trusting.—41, 102, 166, 205, 222.

Victory.—62, 146, 148, 175, 213, 248, 254.

Warning.—82, 116, 132, 135, 136, 212, 214, 237, 251, 267, 269.

Work.—7, 19, 23, 24, 26, 33, 50, 69, 70, 77, 93, 110, 116, 126, 130, 134, 152, 162, 172, 193, 194, 196, 218, 221, 241, 244, 264, 268.

Worship.—144, 145, 147, 150, 154, 156, 166, 183, 211, 219, 231, 232, 234, 236, 240, 242, 244, 246, 252, 256.

Young Peoples' Societies.—33, 39, 40, 42, 43, 46, 49, 50, 52, 54, 58, 59, 60, 62, 64, 66, 68, 71, 78, 93, 94, 96, 100, 105, 110, 121, 125, 131, 139, 140, 146, 148, 151, 154, 158, 166, 170, 172, 173, 174, 175, 177, 182, 189, 192, 193, 194, 196, 198, 200, 202, 208, 210, 213, 216, 258, 260, 263, 264, 267, 269, 271.

Glory, Hallelujah!

Rev. D. Williams.

1. On the mountain top of vis-ion, what a glo-ry we be-hold! A hundred years of vic-to-ry are tinging earth with gold; And the glorious time is coming which the prophets long foretold. The Truth is marching on.

Chorus —Glory, glory, hallelujah, &c.

2. For the glory of the Master, Wesley taught beyond the sea,
And preached the great salvation which delivers you and me;
And a million voices shout it,—"Redemption's full and free,"
    Salvation's rolling on.—Glory, glory, hallelujah, &c.

3. From the cabin on the prairie, from the vaulted city dome,
From the dark and briny ocean, where our sailor brothers roam,
We hear the glad rejoicing, like a happy harvest home,
    Salvation's rolling on.—Glory, glory, hallelujah, &c.

4. A hundred years of marching, and a hundred years of song,
The Conqueror advances, and the time will not be long
When he shall claim the heathen and overthrow the wrong,
    Our God is marching on.—Glory, glory, hallelujah, &c.

5. And when the war is over, with the saints forevermore,
On the blissful heights of Glory we will shout the battle o'er,
And in the Golden City we will join the Conqueror,
    Forever marching on.—Glory, glory, hallelujah, &c.

* The Chorus, "Glory, Hallelujah," is so familiar, that the music need not be repeated.

www.ingramcontent.com/pod-product-compliance
Lightning Source LLC
Chambersburg PA
CBHW032150230426
43672CB00011B/2506